PLACE IN RETURN BOX to remove this checkout from your record.
TO AVOID FINES return on or before date due.

DATE DUE	DATE DUE	DATE DUE
OCT 28 1998	DEC 02 2002	
APR 01 2000	OCT 07 2004	
JUL 05 2002		
FEB 18 2006		
DEC 1 6 2006		
APR 1 2 2022 APR 27 2022		

MSU Is An Affirmative Action/Equal Opportunity Institution
c:\circ\datedue.pm3-p.1

Our Blood

Also by Andrea Dworkin: WOMAN HATING

OUR BLOOD

Prophecies and Discourses on Sexual Politics

ANDREA DWORKIN

HARPER & ROW, PUBLISHERS

New York, Hagerstown, San Francisco, London

"Feminism, Art, and My Mother Sylvia." Copyright © 1974 by Andrea Dworkin. First published in *Social Policy*, May/June 1975. Reprinted by permission of the author.

"Renouncing Sexual 'Equality.'" Copyright © 1974 by Andrea Dworkin. First published in *WIN*, October 17, 1974. Reprinted by permission of the author.

"Remembering the Witches." Copyright © 1975 by Andrea Dworkin. First published in *WIN*, February 20, 1975. Reprinted by permission of the author.

"The Rape Atrocity and the Boy Next Door." Copyright © 1975 by Andrea Dworkin. First delivered as a lecture.

"The Sexual Politics of Fear and Courage." Copyright © 1975 by Andrea Dworkin. First delivered as a lecture.

"Redefining Nonviolence." Copyright © 1975 by Andrea Dworkin. Published in *WIN*, July 17, 1975. Delivered as a lecture under the title "A Call to Separatism." Reprinted by permission of the author.

"Lesbian Pride." Copyright © 1975 by Andrea Dworkin. First published under the title "What Is Lesbian Pride?" in *The Second Wave*, Vol. 4, No. 2, 1975. Delivered as a lecture under the title "What Is Lesbian Pride?" Reprinted by permission of the author.

"Our Blood: The Slavery of Women in Amerika." Copyright © 1975 by Andrea Dworkin. First delivered as a lecture under the title "Our Blood."

"The Root Cause." Copyright © 1975 by Andrea Dworkin. First delivered as a lecture under the title "Androgyny."

Grateful acknowledgment is made to Random House, Inc., for permission to reprint from *The Random House Dictionary of the English Language*. Copyright © 1966, 1967 by Random House, Inc.

OUR BLOOD: Prophecies and Discourses on Sexual Politics. Copyright © 1976 by Andrea Dworkin. All rights reserved. Printed in the United States of America. No part of this book may be used or reproduced in any manner whatsoever without written permission except in the case of brief quotations embodied in critical articles and reviews. For information address Harper & Row, Publishers, Inc., 10 East 53rd Street, New York, N.Y. 10022. Published simultaneously in Canada by Fitzhenry & Whiteside Limited, Toronto.

FIRST EDITION

Designed by Dorothy Schmiderer

Library of Congress Cataloging in Publication Data
Dworkin, Andrea.
  Our blood.
  1. Women—Social conditions. 2. Feminism.
I. Title.
HQ1154.D85   1976   301.41′2   76-9187
ISBN 0-06-011116-X

---

76 77 78 79 80 10 9 8 7 6 5 4 3 2 1

Contents

1. Feminism, Art, and My Mother Sylvia   1
2. Renouncing Sexual "Equality"   10
3. Remembering the Witches   15
4. The Rape Atrocity and the Boy Next Door   22
5. The Sexual Politics of Fear and Courage   50
6. Redefining Nonviolence   66
7. Lesbian Pride   73
8. Our Blood: The Slavery of Women in Amerika   76
9. The Root Cause   96

Notes   113

FOR BARBARA DEMING

> I suggest that if we are willing to confront our own most seemingly personal angers, in their raw state, and take upon ourselves the task of translating this raw anger into the disciplined anger of the search for change, we will find ourselves in a position to speak much more persuasively to comrades about the need to root out from all anger the spirit of murder.
>
> Barbara Deming, "On Anger"
> *We Cannot Live Without Our Lives*

IN MEMORY OF SOJOURNER TRUTH

> Now, women do not ask half of a kingdom but their rights, and they don't get them. When she comes to demand them, don't you hear how sons hiss their mothers like snakes, because they ask for their rights; and can they ask for anything less? ... But we'll have our rights; see if we don't; and you can't stop us from them; see if you can. You can hiss as much as you like, but it is coming.
>
> Sojourner Truth, 1853

ACKNOWLEDGMENTS

I thank Kitty Benedict, Phyllis Chesler, Barbara Deming, Jane Gapen, Beatrice Johnson, Eleanor Johnson, Liz Kanegson, Judah Kataloni, Jeanette Koszuth, Elaine Markson, and Joslyn Pine for their help and faith.

I thank John Stoltenberg, who has been my closest intellectual and creative collaborator.

I thank my parents, Sylvia and Harry Dworkin, for their continued trust and respect.

I thank all of the women who organized the conferences, programs, and classes at which I spoke.

I thank those feminist philosophers, writers, organizers, and prophets whose work sustains and strengthens me.

1

Feminism, Art, and My Mother Sylvia

I am very happy to be here today. It is no small thing for me to be here. There are many other places I could be. This is not what my mother had planned for me.

I want to tell you something about my mother. Her name is Sylvia. Her father's name is Spiegel. Her husband's name is Dworkin. She is fifty-nine years old, my mother, and just a few months ago she had a serious heart attack. She is recovered now and back on her job. She is a secretary in a high school. She has been a heart patient most of her life, and all of mine. When she was a child she had rheumatic fever. She says that her real trouble began when she was pregnant with my brother Mark and got pneumonia. After that, her life was a misery of illness. After years of debilitating illness—heart failures, toxic reactions to the drugs that kept her alive—she underwent

Delivered at Smith College, Northampton, Massachusetts, April 16, 1974.

heart surgery, then she suffered a brain clot, a stroke, that robbed her of speech for a long time. She recovered from the heart surgery. She recovered from her stroke, although she still speaks more slowly than she thinks. Then, about eight years ago she had a heart attack. She recovered. Then, a few months ago she had a heart attack. She recovered.

My mother was born in Jersey City, New Jersey, the second oldest of seven children, two boys, five girls. Her parents, Sadie and Edward, who were cousins, came from someplace in Hungary. Her father died before I was born. Her mother is now eighty. There is no way of knowing of course if my mother's heart would have been injured so badly had she been born into a wealthy family. I suspect not, but I do not know. There is also of course no way of knowing if she would have received different medical treatment had she not been a girl. But regardless, it all happened the way it happened, and so she was very ill most of her life. Since she was a girl, no one encouraged her to read books (though she tells me that she used to love to read and does not remember when or why she stopped reading); no one encouraged her to go to college or asked her to consider the problems of the world in which she lived. Because her family was poor, she had to work as soon as she finished high school. She worked as a secretary full-time, and on Saturdays and some evenings she did part-time work as a "salesgirl" in a department store. Then she married my father.

My father was a school teacher and he also worked nights in the post office because he had medical bills to pay. He had to keep my mother alive, and he had two children to support as well. I say along with Joseph Chaikin in *The Presence of the Actor*: "The medical-economic reality in this country is emblematic of the System which literally chooses who is to survive. I renounce my government for its inequitable economic system."*[1] Others, I must point out to you, had and have less than we did. Others who were not my mother but

---
*Notes start on p. 113.

Feminism, Art, and My Mother Sylvia

who were in her situation did and do die. I too renounce this government because the poor die, and they are not only the victims of heart disease, or kidney disease, or cancer—they are the victims of a system which says a visit to the doctor is $25 and an operation is $5,000.

When I was twelve, my mother emerged from her heart surgery and the stroke that had robbed her of speech. There she was, a mother, standing up and giving orders. We had a very hard time with each other. I didn't know who she was, or what she wanted from me. She didn't know who I was, but she had definite ideas about who I should be. She had, I thought, a silly, almost stupid attitude toward the world. By the time I was twelve I knew that I wanted to be a writer or a lawyer. I had been raised really without a mother, and so certain ideas hadn't reached me. I didn't want to be a wife, and I didn't want to be a mother.

My father had really raised me although I didn't see a lot of him. My father valued books and intellectual dialogue. He was the son of Russian immigrants, and they had wanted him to be a doctor. That was their dream. He was a devoted son and so, even though he wanted to study history, he took a pre-medical course in college. He was too squeamish to go through with it all. Blood made him ill. So after pre-med, he found himself, for almost twenty years, teaching science, which he didn't like, instead of history, which he loved. During the years of doing work he disliked, he made a vow that his children would be educated as fully as possible and, no matter what it took from him, no matter what kind of commitment or work or money, his children would become whatever they wanted. My father made his children his art, and he devoted himself to nurturing those children so that they would become whatever they could become. I don't know why he didn't make a distinction between his girl child and his boy child, but he didn't. I don't know why, from the beginning, he gave me books to read, and talked about all of his ideas with me, and watered every ambition that I had so that those ambitions would live and be nourished and grow—but he did.*

So in our household, my mother was out of the running as an influence. My father, whose great love was history, whose commitment was to education and intellectual dialogue, set the tone and taught both my brother and me that our proper engagement was with the world. He had a whole set of ideas and principles that he taught us, in words, by example. He believed, for instance, in racial equality and integration when those beliefs were seen as absolutely aberrational by all of his neighbors, family, and peers. When I, at the age of fifteen, declared to a family gathering that if I wanted to marry I would marry whomever I wanted, regardless of color, my father's answer before that enraged assembly was that he expected no less. He was a civil libertarian. He believed in unions, and fought hard to unionize teachers—an unpopular notion in those days since teachers wanted to see themselves as professionals. He taught us those principles in the Bill of Rights which are now not thought of very highly by most Amerikans—an absolute commitment to free speech in all its forms, equality before just law, and racial equality.

I adored my father, but I had no sympathy for my mother. I knew that she was physically brave—my father told me so over and over—but I didn't see her as any Herculean hero. No woman ever had been, as far as I knew. Her mind was uninteresting. She seemed small and provincial. I remember that once, in the middle of a terrible argument, she said to me in a stony tone of voice: You think I'm stupid. I denied it then, but I know today that she was right. And indeed, what else could one think of a person whose only concern was that I clean up

---

* My mother has reminded me that she introduced me to libraries and that she also always encouraged me to read. I had forgotten this early shared experience because, as I grew older, she and I had some conflicts over the particular books which I insisted on reading, though she never stopped me from reading them. Sometime during my adolescence, books came to connote for me, in part, my intellectual superiority over my mother, who did not read, and my peership with my father, who did read.

my room, or wear certain clothes, or comb my hair another way. I had, certainly, great reason to think that she was stupid, and horrible, and petty, and contemptible even: Edward Albee, Philip Wylie, and that great male artist Sigmund Freud told me so. Mothers, it seemed to me, were the most expendable of people—no one had a good opinion of them, certainly not the great writers of the past, certainly not the exciting writers of the present. And so, though this woman, my mother, whether present or absent, was the center of my life in so many inexplicable, powerful, unchartable ways, I experienced her only as an ignorant irritant, someone without grace or passion or wisdom. When I married in 1969 I felt free—free of my mother, her prejudices, her ignorant demands.

I tell you all of this because this story has, possibly for the first time in history, a rather happier resolution than one might expect.

Do you remember that in Hemingway's *For Whom the Bell Tolls* Maria is asked about her lovemaking with Robert, did the earth move? For me, too, in my life, the earth has sometimes moved. The first time it moved I was ten. I was going to Hebrew school, but it was closed, a day of mourning for the six million slaughtered by the Nazis. So I went to see my cousin who lived nearby. She was shaking, crying, screaming, vomiting. She told me that it was April, and in April her youngest sister had been killed in front of her, another sister's infant had died a terrible death, their heads had been shaved —let me just say that she told me what had happened to her in a Nazi concentration camp. She said that every April she remembered in nightmare and terror what had happened to her that month so many years before, and that every April she shook, cried, screamed, and vomited. The earth moved for me then.

The second time the earth moved for me was when I was eighteen and spent four days in the Women's House of Detention in New York City. I had been arrested in a demonstration against the Indochina genocide. I spent four days and four nights in the filth and terror of that jail. While there two doctors gave me a brutal internal examination. I hemorrhaged for fifteen days after that. The earth moved for me then.

The third time the earth moved for me was when I became a feminist. It wasn't on a particular day, or through one experience. It had to do with that afternoon when I was ten and my cousin put the grief of her life into my hands; it had to do with that women's jail, and three years of marriage that began in friendship and ended in despair. It happened sometime after I left my husband, when I was living in poverty and great emotional distress. It happened slowly, little by little. A week after I left my ex-husband I started my book, the book which is now called *Woman Hating*. I wanted to find out what had happened to me in my marriage and in the thousand and one instances of daily life where it seemed I was being treated like a subhuman. I felt that I was deeply masochistic, but that my masochism was not personal—each woman I knew lived out deep masochism. I wanted to find out why. I knew that I hadn't been taught that masochism by my father, and that my mother had not been my immediate teacher. So I began in what seemed the only apparent place—with *Story of O*, a book that had moved me profoundly. From that beginning I looked at other pornography, fairy tales, one thousand years of Chinese footbinding, and the slaughter of nine million witches. I learned something about the nature of the world which had been hidden from me before—I saw a systematic despisal of women that permeated every institution of society, every cultural organ, every expression of human being. And I saw that I was a woman, a person who met that systematic despisal on every street corner, in every living room, in every human interchange. Because I became a woman who knew that she was a woman, that is, because I became a feminist, I began to speak with women for the first time in my life, and one of the women I began to speak with was my mother. I came to her life through the long dark tunnel of my own. I began to see who she was as I began to see the world that had formed her. I came to her no longer pitying the poverty of her intellect, but astounded by the quality of her intelligence. I came to her no longer convinced of her stupidity and triviality, but astonished by the quality of her strength. I came to her, no longer self-righteous and superior, but as a sister, another woman whose life, but for the grace of a feminist father and the new common struggle of my feminist sisters, would have repeated hers—and when I say "repeated hers" I mean, been predetermined as hers was predetermined. I came to her, no longer ashamed of what she lacked, but deeply proud of what she had achieved—indeed, I came to recognize that my mother was proud, strong, and honest. By the time I was twenty-six I had seen enough of the world and its troubles to know that pride, strength, and integrity were virtues to honor. And because I addressed her in a new way she came to meet me, and now, whatever our difficulties, and they are not so many, she is my mother, and I am her daughter, and we are sisters.

You asked me to talk about feminism and art, is there a feminist art, and if so, what is it. For however long writers have written, until today, there has been masculinist art—art that serves men in a world made by men. That art has degraded women. It has, almost without exception, characterized us as maimed beings, impoverished sensibilities, trivial people with trivial concerns. It has, almost without exception, been saturated with a misogyny so profound, a misogyny that was in fact its world view, that almost all of us, until today, have thought, that is what the world is, that is how women are.

I ask myself, what did I learn from all those books I read as I was growing up? Did I learn anything real or true about women? Did I learn anything real or true about centuries of women and what they lived? Did those books illuminate my life, or life itself, in any useful, or profound, or generous, or rich, or textured, or real way? I do not think so. I think that that art, those books, would have robbed me of my life as the world they served robbed my mother of hers.

Theodore Roethke, a great poet we are told, a poet of the male condition I would insist, wrote:

> Two of the charges most frequently levelled against poetry by women are lack of range—in subject matter, in emotional tone—and lack of a sense of humor. And one could, in individual instances among writers of real talent, add other aesthetic and moral shortcomings: the spinning-out; the embroidering of trivial themes; a concern with the mere surfaces of life—that special province of the feminine talent in prose—hiding from the real agonies of the spirit; refusing to face up to what existence is; lyric or religious posturing; running between the boudoir and the altar, stamping a tiny foot against God; or lapsing into a sententiousness that implies the author has re-invented integrity; carrying on excessively about Fate, about time; lamenting the lot of woman . . . and so on.[2]

What characterizes masculinist art, and the men who make it, is misogyny—and in the face of that misogyny, someone had better reinvent integrity.

They, the masculinists, have told us that they write about the human condition, that their themes are the great themes—love, death, heroism, suffering, history itself. They have told us that our themes—love, death, heroism, suffering, history itself—are trivial because we are, by our very nature, trivial.

I renounce masculinist art. It is not art which illuminates the human condition—it illuminates only, and to men's final and everlasting shame, the masculinist world—and as we look around us, that world is not one to be proud of. Masculinist art, the art of centuries of men, is not universal, or the final explication of what being in the world is. It is, in the end, descriptive only of a world in which women are subjugated, submissive, enslaved, robbed of full becoming, distinguished only by carnality, demeaned. I say, my life is not trivial; my sensibility is not trivial; my struggle is not trivial. Nor was my mother's, or her mother's before her. I renounce those who hate women, who have contempt for women, who ridicule and demean women, and when I do, I renounce most of the art, masculinist art, ever made.

As feminists, we inhabit the world in a new way. We see the world in a new way. We threaten to turn it upside down and inside out. We intend to change it so totally that someday the texts of masculinist writers will be anthropological curiosities. What was that Mailer talking about, our descendants will ask, should they come upon his work in some obscure archive. And they will wonder—bewildered, sad—at the masculinist glorification of war; the masculinist mystifications around killing, maiming, violence, and pain; the tortured masks of phallic heroism; the vain arrogance of phallic supremacy; the impoverished renderings of mothers and daughters, and so of life itself. They will ask, did those people really believe in those gods?

Feminist art is not some tiny creek running off the great river of real art. It is not some crack in an otherwise flawless stone. It is, quite spectacularly I think, art which is not based on the subjugation of one half of the species. It is art which will take the great human themes—love, death, heroism, suffering, history itself—and render them fully human. It may also, though perhaps our imaginations are so mutilated now that we are incapable even of the ambition, introduce a new theme, one as great and as rich as those others—should we call it "joy"?

We cannot imagine a world in which women are not experienced as trivial and contemptible, in which women are not demeaned, abused, exploited, raped, diminished before we are even born—and so we cannot know what kind of art will be made in that new world. Our work, which does full honor to those centuries of sisters who went before us, is to midwife that new world into being. It will be left to our children and their children to live in it.

2

Renouncing Sexual "Equality"

Equality: 1. the state of being equal; correspondence in quantity, degree, value, rank, ability, etc. 2. uniform character, as of motion or surface.

Freedom: 1. state of being at liberty rather than in confinement or under physical restraint . . . 2. exemption from external control, interference, regulation, etc. 3. power of determining one's or its own action . . . 4. *Philos.* the power to make one's own choices or decisions without constraint from within or without; autonomy, self-determination . . . 5. civil liberty, as opposed to subjection to an arbitrary or despotic government. 6. political or national independence . . . 8. personal liberty, as opposed to bondage or slavery . . .

—*Syn.* FREEDOM, INDEPENDENCE, LIBERTY refer to an absence of undue restrictions and an opportunity to exercise one's rights and powers. FREEDOM emphasizes the opportunity given for the exercise of one's rights, powers, desires, or the like . . . INDEPENDENCE implies not only lack of restrictions but also the ability to stand alone, unsustained by anything else . . .

—*Ant.* 1-3. restraint. 5,6,8. oppression.

Justice: 1. the quality of being just; righteousness, equitableness, or moral rightness . . . 2. rightfulness or lawfulness . . . 3. the moral principle determining just conduct. 4. conformity to this principle, as manifested in conduct; just conduct, dealing, or treatment . . .

from *The Random House Dictionary*
of the English Language

In 1970 Kate Millett published *Sexual Politics*. In that book she proved to many of us—who would have staked our lives

Delivered at the National Organization for Women Conference on Sexuality, New York City, October 12, 1974.

on denying it—that sexual relations, the literature depicting those relations, the psychology posturing to explain those relations, the economic systems that fix the necessities of those relations, the religious systems that seek to control those relations, are *political*. She showed us that everything that happens to a woman in her life, everything that touches or molds her, is *political*.[1]

Women who are feminists, that is, women who grasped her analysis and saw that it explained much of their real existence in their real lives, have tried to understand, struggle against, and transform the political system called patriarchy which exploits our labor, predetermines the ownership of our bodies, and diminishes our selfhood from the day we are born. This struggle has no dimension to it which is abstract: it has touched us in every part of our lives. But nowhere has it touched us more vividly or painfully than in that part of our human lives which we call "love" and "sex." In the course of our struggle to free ourselves from systematic oppression, a serious argument has developed among us, and I want to bring that argument into this room.

Some of us have committed ourselves in all areas, including those called "love" and "sex," to the goal of *equality*, that is, to the state of being equal; correspondence in quantity, degree, value, rank, ability; uniform character, as of motion or surface. Others of us, and I stand on this side of the argument, do not see equality as a proper, or sufficient, or moral, or honorable final goal. We believe that to be equal where there is not universal justice, or where there is not universal freedom is, quite simply, to be the same as the oppressor. It is to have achieved "uniform character, as of motion or surface."

Nowhere is this clearer than in the area of sexuality. The male sexual model is based on a polarization of humankind into man/woman, master/slave, aggressor/victim, active/passive. This male sexual model is now many thousands of years old. The very identity of men, their civil and economic power, the forms of government that they have developed, the wars they wage, are tied *irrevocably* together. All forms of dominance and submission, whether it be man over woman, white over black, boss over worker, rich over poor, are tied *irrevocably* to the sexual identities of men and are derived from the male sexual model. Once we grasp this, it becomes clear that *in fact* men own the sex act, the language which describes sex, the women whom they objectify. Men have written the scenario for any sexual fantasy you have ever had or any sexual act you have ever engaged in.

There is no *freedom* or *justice* in exchanging the female role for the male role. There is, no doubt about it, equality. There is no *freedom* or *justice* in using male language, the language of your oppressor, to describe sexuality. There is no *freedom* or *justice* or even common sense in developing a male sexual sensibility—a sexual sensibility which is aggressive, competitive, objectifying, quantity oriented. There is only equality. To believe that freedom or justice for women, or for any individual woman, can be found in mimicry of male sexuality is to delude oneself and to contribute to the oppression of one's sisters.

Many of us would like to think that in the last four years, or ten years, we have reversed, or at least impeded, those habits and customs of the thousands of years which went before—the habits and customs of male dominance. There is no fact or figure to bear that out. You may feel better, or you may not, but statistics show that women are poorer than ever, that women are raped more and murdered more. I want to suggest to you that a commitment to sexual equality with males, that is, to uniform character as of motion or surface, is a commitment to becoming the rich instead of the poor, the rapist instead of the raped, the murderer instead of the murdered. I want to ask you to make a different commitment—a commitment to the abolition of poverty, rape, and murder; that is, a commitment to ending the system of oppression called patriarchy; to ending the male sexual model itself.

The real core of the feminist vision, its revolutionary kernel if you will, has to do with the abolition of all sex roles—that

Renouncing Sexual "Equality"

is, an absolute transformation of human sexuality and the institutions derived from it. In this work, *no part of the male sexual model can possibly apply*. Equality within the framework of the male sexual model, however that model is reformed or modified, can only perpetuate the model itself and the injustice and bondage which are its intrinsic consequences.

I suggest to you that transformation of the male sexual model under which we now all labor and "love" begins where there is a *congruence*, not a separation, a *congruence* of feeling and erotic interest; that it begins in what we do know about female sexuality *as distinct* from male—clitoral touch and sensitivity, multiple orgasms, erotic sensitivity all over the body (which needn't—and shouldn't—be localized or contained genitally), in tenderness, in self-respect and in absolute mutual respect. For men I suspect that this transformation begins in the place they most dread—that is, in a limp penis. I think that men will have to give up their precious erections and begin to make love as women do together. I am saying that men will have to renounce their phallocentric personalities, and the privileges and powers given to them at birth as a consequence of their anatomy, that they will have to excise everything in them that they now value as distinctively "male." No reform, or matching of orgasms, will accomplish this.

I have been reading excerpts from the diary of Sophie Tolstoy, which I found in a beautiful book called *Revelations: Diaries of Women*, edited by Mary Jane Moffat and Charlotte Painter. Sophie Tolstoy wrote:

> And the main thing is not to love. See what I have done by loving him so deeply! It is so painful and humiliating; but he thinks that it is merely silly. "You say one thing and always do another." But what is the good of arguing in this superior manner, when I have nothing in me but this humiliating love and a bad temper; and these two things have been the cause of all my misfortunes, for my temper has always interfered with my love. I want nothing but his love and sympathy, and he won't give it to me; and all my pride is trampled in the mud; I am nothing but a miser-

able crushed worm, whom no one wants, whom no one loves, a useless creature with morning sickness, and a big belly, two rotten teeth, and a bad temper, a battered sense of dignity, and a love which nobody wants and which nearly drives me insane.[2]

Does anyone really think that things have changed so much since Sophie Tolstoy made that entry in her diary on October 25, 1886? And what would you tell her if she came here today, to her sisters? Would you have handed her a vibrator and taught her how to use it? Would you have given her the techniques of fellatio that might better please Mr. Tolstoy? Would you have suggested to her that her salvation lay in becoming a "sexual athlete"? Learning to cruise? Taking as many lovers as Leo did? Would you tell her to start thinking of herself as a "person" and not as a woman?

Or might you have found the courage, the resolve, the conviction to be her true sisters—to help her to extricate herself from the long darkness of Leo's shadow; to join with her in changing the very organization and texture of this world, still constructed in 1974 to serve him, to force her to serve him?

I suggest to you that Sophie Tolstoy is here today, in the bodies and lives of many sisters. Do not fail her.

3

Remembering the Witches

I dedicate this talk to Elizabeth Gould Davis, author of *The First Sex*, who several months ago killed herself and who toward the end of her life was a victim of rape; to Anne Sexton, poet, who killed herself on October 4, 1974; to Inez García, thirty years old, wife and mother, who was a few weeks ago sentenced in California to five years to life imprisonment for killing the three-hundred-pound man who held her down while another man raped her; and to Eva Diamond, twenty-six years old, whose child was taken from her five years ago when she was declared an unfit mother because she was convicted of welfare fraud and who several months ago was sentenced in Minnesota to fifteen years in prison for killing her husband of one year while he was attempting to beat her to death.

Delivered at New York City chapter meeting of the National Organization for Women, October 31, 1974.

We are here tonight to talk about gynocide. Gynocide is the systematic crippling, raping, and/or killing of women by men. Gynocide is the word that designates the relentless violence perpetrated by the gender class men against the gender class women.

For instance, Chinese footbinding is an example of gynocide. For one thousand years in China all women were systematically crippled so that they would be passive, erotic objects for men; so that they were carnal property; so that they were entirely dependent on men for food, water, shelter, and clothing; so that they could not walk, or walk away, or unite against the sadism of their male oppressors.

Another example of gynocide is the systematic rape of the women of Bangladesh. There, the rape of women was part of the military strategy of the male invading armies. As many of you know, it is estimated that between 200,000 and 400,000 women were raped by the invading soldiers and when the war was over, those women were considered unclean by their husbands, brothers, and fathers, and were left to whore, starve, and die. The Bangladesh gynocide was perpetrated first by the men who invaded Bangladesh, and then by those who lived there—the husbands, brothers, and fathers: it was perpetrated by the gender class men against the gender class women.

Tonight, on Halloween, we are here to remember another gynocide, the mass slaughter of the nine million women who were called witches. These women, our sisters, were killed over a period of three hundred years in Germany, Spain, Italy, France, Holland, Switzerland, England, Wales, Ireland, Scotland, and Amerika. They were killed in the name of God the Father and His only Son, Jesus Christ.

The organized persecution of the witches began officially on December 9, 1484. Pope Innocent VIII named two Dominican monks, Heinrich Kramer and James Sprenger, as Inquisitors and asked the good fathers to define witchcraft, to isolate the *modus operandi* of the witches, and to standardize trial procedures and sentencing. Kramer and Sprenger wrote a text called the *Malleus Maleficarum*. The *Malleus Maleficarum* was high Catholic theology and working Catholic jurisprudence. It might be compared to the Amerikan Constitution. It was the law. Anyone who challenged it was guilty of heresy, a capital crime. Anyone who refuted its authority or questioned its credibility on any level was guilty of heresy, a capital crime.

Before I discuss the content of the *Malleus Maleficarum*, I want to be clear about the statistical information that we do have on the witches. The total figure of nine million is a moderate one. It is the figure most often used by scholars in the field. The ratio of women to men burned is variously estimated at 20 to 1 and 100 to 1.

Witchcraft was a woman's crime, and much of the text of the *Malleus* explains why. First, Jesus Christ was born, suffered, and died to save *men*, not women; therefore, women were more vulnerable to Satan's enticements. Second, a woman is "more carnal than a man, as is clear from her many carnal abominations."[1] This excess of carnality originated in Eve's very creation: she was formed from a bent rib. Because of this defect, women always deceive. Third, women are, by definition, wicked, malicious, vain, stupid, and irredeemably evil: "I had rather dwell with a lion and a dragon than to keep house with a wicked woman. . . . All wickedness is but little to the wickedness of a woman . . . When a woman thinks alone, she thinks evil."[2] Fourth, women are weaker than men in both mind and body and are intellectually like children. Fifth, women are "more bitter than death" because all sin originates in and on account of women, and because women are "wheedling and secret" enemies.[3] Finally, witchcraft was a woman's crime because "All witchcraft comes from carnal lust, which is in women insatiable."[4]

I want you to remember that these are not the polemics of aberrants; these are the convictions of scholars, lawmakers, judges. I want you to remember that nine million women were burned alive.

Witches were accused of flying, having carnal relations with

Satan, injuring cattle, causing hailstorms and tempests, causing illnesses and epidemics, bewitching men, changing men and themselves into animals, changing animals into people, committing acts of cannibalism and murder, stealing male genitals, causing male genitals to disappear. In fact, this last—causing male genitals to disappear—was grounds under Catholic law for divorce. If a man's genitals were invisible for more than three years, his spouse was entitled to a divorce.

It would be hard to locate in Sprenger and Kramer's gargantuan mass of woman-hating the most odious charge, the most incredible charge, the most ridiculous charge, but I do think that I have done it. Sprenger and Kramer wrote:

> And what, then, is to be thought of those witches who . . . collect male organs in great numbers, as many as twenty or thirty members together, and put them in a bird's nest, or shut them up in a box, where they move themselves like living members, and eat oats and corn, as has been seen by many and is a matter of common report?[5]

What indeed? What are we to think? What are those of us who grew up Catholics, for instance, to think? When we see that priests are performing exorcisms in Amerikan suburbs, that the belief in witchcraft is still a fundament of Catholic theology, what are we to think? When we discover that Luther energized this gynocide through his many confrontations with Satan, what are we to think? When we discover that Calvin himself burned witches, and that he personally supervised the witch hunts in Zurich, what are we to think? When we discover that the fear and loathing of female carnality are codified in Jewish law, what are we to think?

Some of us have a very personal view of the world. We say that what happens to us in our lives as women happens to us as individuals. We even say that any violence we have experienced in our lives as women—for instance, rape or assault by a husband, lover, or stranger—happened between two individuals. Some of us even apologize for the aggressor—we feel sorry for him; we say that he is personally disturbed, or that he was provoked in a particular way, at a particular time, by a particular woman.

Men tell us that they too are "oppressed." They tell us that they are often in their individual lives victimized by women—by mothers, wives, and "girlfriends." They tell us that women provoke acts of violence through our carnality, or malice, or avarice, or vanity, or stupidity. They tell us that their violence originates in us and that we are responsible for it. They tell us that their lives are full of pain, and that we are its source. They tell us that as mothers we injure them irreparably, as wives we castrate them, as lovers we steal from them semen, youth, and manhood—and never, never, as mothers, wives, or lovers do we ever give them enough.

And what are we to think? Because if we begin to piece together all of the instances of violence—the rapes, the assaults, the cripplings, the killings, the mass slaughters; if we read their novels, poems, political and philosophical tracts and see that they think of us today what the Inquisitors thought of us yesterday; if we realize that historically gynocide is not some mistake, some accidental excess, some dreadful fluke, but is instead the logical consequence of what they believe to be our god-given or biological natures; then we must finally understand that under patriarchy gynocide is the ongoing reality of life lived by women. And then we must look to each other—for the courage to bear it and for the courage to change it.

The struggle of women, the feminist struggle, is not a struggle for more money per hour, or for equal rights under male law, or for more women legislators who will operate within the confines of male law. These are all emergency measures, designed to save women's lives, as many as possible, now, today. But these reforms will not stem the tide of gynocide; these reforms will not end the relentless violence perpetrated by the gender class men against the gender class women. These reforms will not stop the increasing rape epidemic in this country, or the wife-beating epidemic in England. They will not stop the sterilizations of black and poor white women who are the victims of male doctors who hate female carnality. These reforms will not empty mental institutions of women put into them by male relatives who hate them for rebelling against the limits of the female role, or against the conditions of female servitude. They will not empty prisons filled with women who, in order to survive, whored; or who, after being raped, killed the rapist; or who, while being beaten, killed the man who was killing them. These reforms will not stop men from living off exploited female domestic labor, nor will these reforms stop men from reinforcing male identity by psychologically victimizing women in so-called "love" relationships.

And no personal accommodation within the system of patriarchy will stop this relentless gynocide. Under patriarchy, no woman is safe to live her life, or to love, or to mother children. Under patriarchy, every woman is a victim, past, present, and future. Under patriarchy, every woman's daughter is a victim, past, present, and future. Under patriarchy, every woman's son is her potential betrayer and also the inevitable rapist or exploiter of another woman.

Before we can live and love, we will have to hone ourselves into a revolutionary sisterhood. That means that we must stop supporting the men who oppress us; that we must refuse to feed and clothe and clean up after them; that we must refuse to let them take their sustenance from our lives. That means that we will have to divest ourselves of the identity we have been trained to as females—that we will have to divest ourselves of all traces of the masochism we have been told is synonymous with being female. That means that we will have to attack and destroy every institution, law, philosophy, religion, custom, and habit of this patriarchy—this patriarchy that feeds on our "dirty" blood, that is built on our "trivial" labor.

Halloween is the appropriate time to commit ourselves to this revolutionary sisterhood. On this night we remember our dead. On this night we remember together that nine million women were killed because men said that they were carnal, malicious, and wicked. On this night we know that they live now through us.

Let us together rename this night Witches' Eve. Let us together make it a time of mourning: for all women who are victims of gynocide, dead, in jail, in mental institutions, raped, sterilized against their wills, brutalized. And let us on this night consecrate our lives to developing the revolutionary sisterhood—the political strategies, the feminist actions—which will stop for all time the devastating violence against us.

4

The Rape Atrocity
and the Boy Next Door

I want to talk to you about rape—*rape*—what it is, who does it, to whom it is done, how it is done, why it is done, and what to do about it so that it will not be done any more.

First, though, I want to make a few introductory remarks.* From 1964 to 1965 and from 1966 to 1968, I went to Bennington College in Vermont. Bennington at that time was still a women's school, or, as people said then, a girls' school. It was a very insular place—entirely isolated from the Vermont

Delivered at State University of New York at Stony Brook, March 1, 1975; University of Pennsylvania, April 25, 1975; State University of New York College at Old Westbury, May 10, 1975; Womanbooks, New York City, July 1, 1975; Woodstock Women's Center, Woodstock, New York, July 3, 1975; Suffolk County Community College, October 9, 1975; Queens College, City University of New York, April 26, 1976.

* These introductory remarks were delivered only at schools where there was no women's studies program.

community in which it was situated, exclusive, expensive. There was a small student body highly concentrated in the arts, a low student-faculty ratio, and an apocryphal tradition of intellectual and sexual "freedom." In general, Bennington was a very distressing kind of playpen where wealthy young women were educated to various accomplishments which would insure good marriages for the respectable and good affairs for the bohemians. At that time, there was more actual freedom for women at Bennington than at most schools—in general, we could come and go as we liked, whereas most other schools had rigid curfews and controls; and in general we could wear what we wanted, whereas in most other schools women still had to conform to rigid dress codes. We were encouraged to read and write and make pots, and in general to take ourselves seriously, even though the faculty did not take us seriously at all. Being better educated to reality than we were, they, the faculty, knew what we did not imagine— that most of us would take our highfalutin ideas about James and Joyce and Homer and invest them in marriages and volunteer work. Most of us, as the mostly male faculty knew, would fall by the wayside into silence and all our good intentions and vast enthusiasms had nothing to do with what would happen to us once we left that insulated playpen. At the time I went to Bennington, there was no feminist consciousness there or anywhere else at all. Betty Friedan's *The Feminine Mystique* concerned housewives—we thought that it had nothing to do with us. Kate Millett's *Sexual Politics* was not yet published. Shulamith Firestone's *The Dialectic of Sex* was not yet published. We were in the process of becoming very well-educated women—we were already very privileged women—and yet not many of us had ever heard the story of the movement for women's suffrage in this country or Europe. In the Amerikan history courses I took, women's suffrage was not mentioned. The names of Angelina and Sarah Grimké, or Susan B. Anthony, or Elizabeth Cady Stanton, were never mentioned. Our ignorance was so complete that we did not know that we had been consigned from birth to that living legal and social death called marriage. We imagined, in our ignorance, that we might be novelists and philosophers. A rare few among us even aspired to be mathematicians and biologists. We did not know that our professors had a system of beliefs and convictions that designated us as an *inferior gender class*, and that that system of beliefs and convictions was virtually universal—the cherished assumption of most of the writers, philosophers, and historians we were so ardently studying. We did not know, for instance, to pick an obvious example, that our Freudian psychology professor believed along with Freud that "the effect of penis-envy has a share . . . in the physical vanity of women, since they are bound to value their charms more highly as a late compensation for their original sexual inferiority."[1] In each field of study, such convictions were central, underlying, crucial. And yet we did not know that *they* meant *us*. This was true everywhere where women were being educated.

As a result, women of my age left colleges and universities completely ignorant of what one might call "real life." We did not know that we would meet everywhere a systematic despisal of our intelligence, creativity, and strength. We did not know our herstory as a gender class. We did not know that we were a gender class, inferior by law and custom to men who were defined, by themselves and all the organs of their culture, as supreme. We did not know that we had been trained all our lives to be victims—inferior, submissive, passive objects who could lay no claim to a discrete individual identity. We did not know that because we were women our labor would be exploited wherever we worked—in jobs, in political movements —by men for their own self-aggrandizement. We did not know that all our hard work in whatever jobs or political movements would never advance our responsibilities or our rewards. We did not know that we were there, wherever, to cook, to do menial labor, to be fucked.

I tell you this now because this is what I remembered

when I knew I would come here to speak tonight. I imagine that in some ways it is different for you. There is an astounding feminist literature to educate you even if your professors will not. There are feminist philosophers, poets, comedians, herstorians, and politicians who are creating feminist culture. There is your own feminist consciousness, which you must nurture, expand, and deepen at every opportunity.

As of now, however, there is no women's study program here. The development of such a program is essential to you as women. Systematic and rigorous study of woman's place in this culture will make it possible for you to understand the world as it acts on and affects you. Without that study, you will leave here as I left Bennington—ignorant of what it means to be a woman in a patriarchal society—that is, in a society where women are systematically defined as inferior, where women are systematically despised.

I am here tonight to try to tell you as much as I can about what you are up against as women in your efforts to live decent, worthwhile, and productive human lives. And that is why I chose tonight to speak about rape which is, though no contemporary Amerikan male writer will tell you so, the dirtiest four-letter word in the English language. Once you understand what rape is, you will understand the forces that systematically oppress you as women. Once you understand what rape is, you will be able to begin the work of changing the values and institutions of this patriarchal society so that you will not be oppressed anymore. Once you understand what rape is, you will be able to resist all attempts to mystify and mislead you into believing that the crimes committed against you as women are trivial, comic, irrelevant. Once you understand what rape is, you will find the resources to take your lives as women seriously and to organize as women against the persons and institutions which demean and violate you.

The word *rape* comes from the Latin word *rapere*, which means "to steal, seize, or carry away."

The first definition of rape in *The Random House Dictionary* is still "the act of seizing and carrying off by force."

The second definition, with which you are probably familiar, defines rape as "the act of physically forcing a woman to have sexual intercourse."

For the moment, I will refer exclusively to the first definition of rape, that is, "the act of seizing and carrying off by force."

Rape precedes marriage, engagement, betrothal, and courtship as sanctioned social behavior. In the bad old days, when a man wanted a woman he simply took her—that is, he abducted and fucked her. The *abduction*, which was always for sexual purposes, was the rape. If the raped woman pleased the rapist, he kept her. If not, he discarded her.

Women, in those bad old days, were chattel. That is, women were property, owned objects, to be bought, sold, used, and stolen—that is, raped. A woman belonged first to her father who was her patriarch, her master, her lord. The very derivation of the word *patriarchy* is instructive. *Pater* means owner, possessor, or master. The basic social unit of patriarchy is the family. The word *family* comes from the Oscan *famel*, which means servant, slave, or possession. *Paterfamilias* means owner of slaves. The rapist who abducted a woman took the place of her father as her owner, possessor, or master.

The Old Testament is eloquent and precise in delineating the right of a man to rape. Here, for instance, is Old Testament law on the rape of enemy women. Deuteronomy, Chapter 21, verses 10 to 15—

> When you go to war against your enemies and Yahweh your God delivers them into your power and you take prisoners, if you see a beautiful woman among the prisoners and find her desirable, you may make her your wife and bring her to your home. She is to shave her head and cut her nails and take off her prisoner's garb; she is to stay inside your house and must mourn her father and mother for a full month. Then you may go to her and be a

husband to her, and she shall be your wife. Should she cease to please you, you will let her go where she wishes, not selling her for money; you are not to make any profit out of her, since you have had the use of her.[2]

A discarded woman, of course, was a pariah or a whore.

Rape, then, is the first model for marriage. Marriage laws sanctified rape by reiterating the right of the rapist to ownership of the raped. Marriage laws protected the property rights of the first rapist by designating a second rapist as an adulterer, that is, a thief. Marriage laws also protected the father's ownership of the daughter. Marriage laws guaranteed the father's right to sell a daughter into marriage, to sell her to another man. Any early strictures against rape were strictures against robbery—against the theft of property. It is in this context, and in this context only, that we can understand rape as a capital crime. This is the Old Testament text on the theft of women as a capital offense. Deuteronomy 22:22 to 23:1—

> If a man is caught sleeping with another man's wife, both must die, the man who has slept with her and the woman herself. You must banish this evil from Israel.
>
> If a virgin is betrothed and a man meets her in the city and sleeps with her, you shall take them both out to the gate of the town and stone them to death; the girl, because she did not cry for help in the town; the man, because he has violated the wife of his fellow. You must banish this evil from your midst. But if the man has met the betrothed girl in the open country and has taken her by force and lain with her, only the man who lay with her shall die; you must do nothing to the girl, for hers is no capital offence. The case is like that of a man who attacks and kills his fellow; for he came across her in the open country and the betrothed girl could have cried out without anyone coming to her rescue.
>
> If a man meets a virgin who is not betrothed and seizes her and lies with her and is caught in the act, the man who has lain with her must give the girl's father fifty silver shekels; she shall be his wife since he has violated her, and as long as he lives he may not repudiate her.

A man must not take his father's wife, and must not withdraw the skirt of his father's cloak from her.[3]

Women belonged to men; the laws of marriage sanctified that ownership; rape was the theft of a woman from her owner. These biblical laws are the basis of the social order as we know it. They have not to this day been repudiated.

As history advanced, men escalated their acts of aggression against women and invented many myths about us to insure both ownership and easy sexual access. In 500 B.C. Herodotus, the so-called Father of History, wrote: "Abducting young women is not, indeed, a lawful act; but it is stupid after the event to make a fuss about it. The only sensible thing is to take no notice; for it is obvious that no young woman allows herself to be abducted if she does not wish to be."[4] Ovid in the *Ars amatoria* wrote: "Women often wish to give unwillingly what they really like to give."[5] And so, it became official: women want to be raped.

Early English law on rape was a testament to the English class system. A woman who was not married belonged legally to the king. Her rapist had to pay the king fifty shillings as a fine, but if she was a "grinding slave," then the fine was reduced to twenty-five shillings. The rape of a nobleman's serving maid cost twelve shillings. The rape of a commoner's serving maid cost five shillings. But if a slave raped a commoner's serving maid, he was castrated. And if he raped any woman of higher rank, he was killed.[6] Here, too, rape was a crime against the man who owned the woman.

Even though rape is sanctioned in the Bible, even though the Greeks had glorified rape—remember Zeus' interminable adventures—and even though Ovid had waxed euphoric over rape, it was left to Sir Thomas Malory to popularize rape for us English-speaking folk. *Le Morte d'Arthur* is the classic work on courtly love. It is a powerful romanticization of rape. Malory is the direct literary ancestor of those modern male Amerikan writers who postulate rape as mythic lovemaking. A good woman is to be taken, possessed by a gallant knight, sexually forced into a submissive passion which would, by male definition, become her delight. Here rape is transformed, or mystified, into romantic love. Here rape becomes the signet of romantic love. Here we find the first really modern rendering of rape: sometimes a woman is seized and carried off; sometimes she is sexually forced and left, madly, passionately in love with the rapist who is, by virtue of an excellent rape, her owner, her love. (Malory, by the way, was arrested and charged with raping, on two separate occasions, a married woman, Joan Smyth.)[7] In his work, rape is no longer synonymous with abduction—it has now become synonymous with love. At issue, of course, is still male ownership—the rapist owns the woman; but now, she loves him as well.

This motif of sexual relating—that is, rape—remains our primary model for heterosexual relating. The dictionary defines rape as "the act of physically forcing a woman to have sexual intercourse." But in fact, rape, in our system of masculinist law, remains a right of marriage. A man cannot be convicted of raping his own wife. In all fifty states, rape is defined legally as forced penetration by a man of a woman "not his wife."[8] When a man forcibly penetrates his own wife, he has not committed a crime of theft against another man. Therefore, according to masculinist law, he has not raped. And, of course, a man cannot abduct his own wife since she is required by law to inhabit his domicile and submit to him sexually. Marriage remains, in our time, carnal *ownership* of women. A man cannot be prosecuted for using his own property as he sees fit.

In addition, rape is our primary emblem of romantic love. Our modern writers, from D. H. Lawrence to Henry Miller to Norman Mailer to Ayn Rand, consistently present rape as the means of introducing a woman to her own carnality. A woman is taken, possessed, conquered by brute force—and it is the rape itself that transforms her into a carnal creature. It is the rape itself which defines both her identity and her function: she is a woman, and as a woman she exists to be fucked.

In masculinist terms, a woman can never be raped against her will since the notion is that if she does not want to be raped, she does not know her will.

Rape, in our society, is still not viewed as a crime against women. In "Forcible and Statutory Rape: An Exploration of the Operation and Objectives of the Consent Standard," *The Yale Law Journal*, 1952, an article which is a relentless compendium of misogynistic slander, the intent of modern male jurisprudence in the area of criminal rape is articulated clearly: the laws exist to protect men (1) from the false accusation of rape (which is taken to be the most likely type of accusation) and (2) from the theft of female property, or its defilement, by another man.[9] The notion of consent to sexual intercourse as the inalienable human right of a woman does not exist in male jurisprudence; a woman's withholding of consent is seen only as a socially appropriate form of barter and the notion of consent is honored only insofar as it protects the male's proprietary rights to her body:

> The consent standard in our society does more than protect a significant item of social currency for women; it fosters, and is in turn bolstered by, a masculine pride in the exclusive possession of a sexual object. The consent of a woman to sexual intercourse awards the man a privilege of bodily access, a personal "prize" whose value is enhanced by sole ownership. . . . An additional reason for the man's condemnation of rape may be found in the threat to his status from a decrease in the "value" of his sexual "possession" which would result from forcible violation.[10]

This remains the basic articulation of rape as a social crime: it is a crime against men, a violation of the male right to personal and exclusive possession of a woman as a sexual object.

Is it any wonder, then, that when Andra Medea and Kathleen Thompson, the authors of *Against Rape*, did a study of women and rape, large numbers of women, when asked, "Have you ever been raped?" answered, "I don't know."[11]

What is rape?

Rape is the first model for marriage. As such, it is sanctioned by the Bible and by thousands of years of law, custom, and habit.

Rape is an act of theft—a man takes the sexual property of another man.

Rape is, by law and custom, a crime against men, against the particular owner of a particular woman.

Rape is the primary heterosexual model for sexual relating.

Rape is the primary emblem of romantic love.

Rape is the means by which a woman is initiated into her womanhood as it is defined by men.

Rape is the right of any man who desires any woman, as long as she is not explicitly owned by another man. This explains clearly why defense lawyers are allowed to ask rape victims personal and intimate questions about their sexual lives. If a woman is a virgin, then she still belongs to her father and a crime has been committed. If a woman is not married and is not a virgin, then she belongs to no particular man and a crime has not been committed.

These are the fundamental cultural, legal, and social assumptions about rape: (1) women want to be raped, in fact, women need to be raped; (2) women provoke rape; (3) no woman can be sexually forced against her will; (4) women love their rapists; (5) in the act of rape, men affirm their own manhood and they also *affirm* the identity and function of women—that is, women exist to be fucked by men and so, in the act of rape, men actually affirm the very womanhood of women. Is it any wonder, then, that there is an epidemic of forcible rape in this country and that most convicted rapists do not know what it is they have done wrong?

In *Beyond God the Father*, Mary Daly says that as women we have been deprived of the power of *naming*.[12] Men, as engineers of this culture, have defined all the words we use. Men, as the makers of law, have defined what is legal and what is not. Men, as the creators of systems of philosophy and morality, have defined what is right and what is wrong. Men, as writers, artists, movie makers, psychologists and psychiatrists, politicians, religious leaders, prophets, and so-called revolutionaries have defined for us who we are, what our values are, how we perceive what happens to us, how we understand what happens to us. At the root of all the definitions they have made is one resolute conviction: that women were put on this earth for the use, pleasure, and sexual gratification of men.

In the case of rape, men have defined for us our function, our value, and the uses to which we may be put.

For women, as Mary Daly says, one fundamental revolutionary act is to reclaim the power of naming, to define for ourselves what our experience is and has been. This is very hard to do. We use a language which is sexist to its core: developed by men in their own interests; formed specifically to exclude us; used specifically to oppress us. The work, then, of naming is crucial to the struggle of women; the work of naming is, in fact, the first revolutionary work we must do. How, then, do *we* define rape?

Rape is a crime against *women*.

Rape is an act of aggression against women.

Rape is a contemptuous and hostile act against women.

Rape is a violation of a woman's right to self-determination.

Rape is a violation of a woman's right to absolute control of her own body.

Rape is an act of sadistic domination.

Rape is a colonializing act.

Rape is a function of male imperialism over and against women.

The crime of rape against one woman is a crime committed against all women.

Generally, we recognize that rape can be divided into two distinct categories: *forcible rape* and *presumptive rape.* In a forcible rape, a man physically assaults a woman and forces her, through physical violence, threat of physical violence, or threat of death, to perform *any* sexual act. *Any* forced sexual act must be considered rape—"contact between the mouth and the anus, the mouth and the penis, the mouth and the vulva, [contact] between the penis and the vulva, [between the] penis and anus, or contact between the anus or vulva" and any phallic substitute like a bottle, stick, or dildo.[13]

In a presumptive rape, we are warranted in presuming that a man has had carnal access to a woman without her consent, because we define *consent* as "meaningful and knowledgeable assent; not mere acquiescence."[14] In a presumptive rape, the constraint on the victim's will is in the circumstance itself; there has been no mutuality of choice and understanding and therefore the basic human rights of the victim have been violated and a crime has been committed against her. This is one instance of presumptive rape, reported by Medea and Thompson in *Against Rape*:

> The woman is seventeen, a high school student. It is about four o'clock in the afternoon. Her boy friend's father has picked her up in his car after school to take her to meet his son. He stops by his house and says she should wait for him in the car. When he has pulled the car into the garage, this thirty-seven-year-old father of six rapes her.[15]

This sort of rape is common, it is contemptible, and needless to say, it is never reported to the police.

Who, then, commits rape?

The fact is that rape is not committed by psychopaths. Rape is committed by normal men. There is nothing, except a conviction for rape which is very hard to obtain, to distinguish the rapist from the nonrapist.

The Institute for Sex Research did a study of rapists in the 1940's and 1950's. In part, the researchers concluded that "... there are no outstandingly ominous signs in [the rapists'] presex-offense histories; indeed, their heterosexual adjustment is quantitatively well above average."[16]

Dr. Menachim Amir, an Israeli criminologist, did an intensive survey of 646 rape cases handled by the Philadelphia Police Department from January to December 1958 and from January to December 1960. In his study, *Patterns of Forcible Rape*, he criticizes psychoanalytic interpretations of rapists' behavior by pointing out that studies "indicate that sex offenders do not constitute a unique clinical or psychopathological type; nor are they as a group invariably more disturbed than the control groups to which they are compared."[17]

Or, as Allan Taylor, a parole officer in California, said: "Those men [convicted rapists] were the most normal men [in prison]. They had a lot of hang-ups, but they were the same hang-ups as men walking out on the street."[18]

In Amir's study, most rapists were between fifteen and nineteen years old. Men twenty to twenty-four constituted the second largest group.[19] In 63.8 percent of the cases, the offender and the victim were in the same age group ($\pm$ 5 years); in 18.6 percent, the victim was at least ten years younger than the offender; in 17.6 percent, the victim was at least ten years older.[20]

The FBI, in its *Uniform Crime Reports*, reported that in 1974, 55,210 women were raped in this country. This was an 8 percent increase over 1973, and a 49 percent increase over 1969. The FBI notes that rape is "probably one of the most under-reported crimes due primarily to fear and/or embarrassment on the part of its victims."[21] Carol V. Horos, in her book *Rape*, estimates that for every rape reported to the police, *ten* are not.[22] Applying Horos' estimate to the number of rapes reported in 1974 brings the total estimate of rapes committed in that year to 607,310. It is important to remember that FBI statistics are based on the male definition of rape, and on the numbers of men arrested and convicted for rape under that definition. According to the FBI, of all those rapes reported to the police in 1974, only 51 percent resulted in arrest, and in only one case out of ten was the rapist finally convicted.[23]

According to Medea and Thompson who studied rape victims, 47 percent of all rapes occurred either in the victim's or the rapist's home; 10 percent occurred in other buildings; 18 percent occurred in cars; 25 percent occurred in streets, alleys, parks, and in the country.[24] Both Amir, who studied rapists, and Medea and Thompson, who studied rape victims, agree that the chances are better than 50 percent that the rapist will be someone the victim knows—someone known by sight, or a neighbor, a fellow worker, a friend, an ex-lover, a date.[25] Medea and Thompson also ascertained that 42 percent of rapists behaved calmly, and that 73 percent used force.[26] In other words, many rapists are calm and use force at the same time.

For us as women, this information is devastating. Over half a million women were raped in this country in 1974, and rape is on the rise. Rapists are normal heterosexual men. At least 50 percent of rape victims will be raped by men they know. In addition, according to Amir, 71 percent of all rapes were fully planned; 11 percent were partially planned; and only 16 percent were unplanned.[27]

Rape has the lowest conviction rate for any violent crime. According to Horos, in 1972 only 133 of every 1,000 men tried for rape were convicted.[28] Medea and Thompson report that juries will acquit nine times out of ten.[29] The reason for this is obvious: the woman is presumed to have provoked the rape and she is held responsible for it. In particular, when the woman knows the rapist, 50 percent of the time, there is virtually no possibility of a conviction.

Who are the victims of rape? Women—of all classes, races, from all walks of life, of all ages. Most rapes are intraracial—that is, white men rape white women and black men rape black women. The youngest rape victim on record is a two-week-old female infant.[30] The oldest rape victim on record is a ninety-three-year-old woman.[31] This is the testimony of a woman who was raped late in life.

> Rape is not an academic question with the present writer, for not long ago (June 4, 1971) she, then in her late fifties, joined the growing army of rape victims. It was a case of forcing a window and entering, forcible assault with the huge bruising hands of the rapist tight around her neck, and was accompanied by burglary.
>
> All these circumstances convinced the police immediately that a crime had been committed. (It helps to be elderly and no longer sexually attractive, too.) . . .
>
> It was 2 or 3 days before the shock wore off and the full impact of the experience hit her. She became very ill, and now, nearly 3 years later, she has not recovered. The police told her she was lucky not to have been murdered. But that remains an unanswered question in her mind. Simple murder would not have involved the horror, the insulting violation of personhood, the degradation, the devastating affront to the dignity, and the sensation of bodily filth that time has not washed off. Nor would it have led to years of startled awakenings from sound sleep, the cold sweats at noises in the dark, the palpitations of the heart at the sound of a deep male voice, the horribly repeated image of two large muscular hands approaching her throat, the rumbling voice that promised to kill her if she struggled or tried to scream, the unbearable vision of being found on the floor of her own home, lying half naked and dead with her legs ridiculously spread.
>
> What was lucky about it was that it happened nearer the end of her life than the beginning. What torture it must be to *young* women who have to live with such memories for fifty years! This older woman's heart goes out to them.[32]

This was the testimony of the great Elizabeth Gould Davis, author of *The First Sex*, who died on July 30, 1974, of a self-inflicted gunshot wound. She had cancer, and she planned her death with great dignity, but I believe that it was the rape, not the cancer, that distressed her unto death.

Now, I could read you testimony after testimony, tell you

story after story—after all, in 1974 there were 607,310 such stories to tell—but I don't think I have to prove to you that rape is a crime of such violence and that it is so rampant that we must view it as an ongoing atrocity against women. All women live in constant jeopardy, in a virtual state of siege. That is, simply, the truth. I do however want to talk to you explicitly about one particularly vicious form of rape which is increasing rapidly in frequency. This is multiple rape—that is, the rape of one woman by two or more men.

In Amir's study of 646 rape cases in Philadelphia in 1958 and 1960, a full 43 percent of all rapes were multiple rapes (16 percent pair rapes, 27 percent group rapes).[33] I want to tell you about two multiple rapes in some detail. The first is reported by Medea and Thompson in *Against Rape*. A twenty-five-year-old woman, mentally retarded, with a mental age of eleven years, lived alone in an apartment in a university town. She was befriended by some men from a campus fraternity. These men took her to the fraternity house, whereupon she was raped by approximately forty men. These men also tried to force intercourse between her and a dog. These men also put bottles and other objects up her vagina. Then, they took her to a police station and charged her with prostitution. Then, they offered to drop the charges against her if she was institutionalized. She was institutionalized; she discovered that she was pregnant; then, she had a complete emotional breakdown.

One man who had been a participant in the rape bragged about it to another man. That man, who was horrified, told a professor. A campus group confronted the fraternity. At first, the accused men admitted that they had committed all the acts charged, but they denied that it was rape since, they claimed, the woman had consented to all of the sexual acts committed. Subsequently, when the story was made public, these same men denied the story completely.

A women's group on campus demanded that the fraternity be thrown off campus to demonstrate that the university did not condone gang rape. No action was taken against the fraternity by university officials or by the police.[34]

The second story that I want to tell was reported by Robert Sam Anson in an article called "That Championship Season" in *New Times* magazine.[35] According to Anson, on July 25, 1974, Notre Dame University suspended for at least one year six black football players for what the university called "a serious violation of university regulations." An eighteen-year-old white high school student, it turned out, had charged the football players with gang rape.

The victim's attorney, the county prosecutor, the local reporter assigned to cover the story, a trustee of the local newspaper—all were Notre Dame alumni, and all helped to cover up the rape charge.

Notre Dame University, according to Anson, has insisted that no crime was committed. It was the consensus of university officials that the football players were just sowing their wild oats in an old-fashioned gang bang, and that the victim was a willing participant. The football players were suspended for having sex in their dormitory. The President of Notre Dame, Theodore H(burgh, a noted liberal and scholar, a Catholic priest, insisted that no rape took place and said that the university would produce, if necessary, "dozens of eyewitnesses." I quote Anson:

> Hesburgh's conclusions are based on an hour-long personal interview with the six football players, along with an investigation conducted by his Dean of Students, John Macheca, a . . . former university public relations man . . . Macheca himself will say nothing about his investigation . . . Various campus sources close to the case say that, throughout his investigation, no university official spoke either to the girl [*sic*] or her parents. Hesburgh himself professes neither to know or to care. He says testily, "It's irrelevant. . . . I didn't need to talk to the girl. I talked to the boys."[36]

According to Anson, had Dr. Hesburgh talked to "the girl" he would have heard this story: after work late on July 3, she went to Notre Dame to see the football player she had been dating; they made love twice on his dormitory bunk; he left the room; she was alone and undressed, wrapped in a sheet; another football player entered the room; she had a history of hostility and confrontation with this second football player (he had made a friend of hers pregnant, he had refused to pay for an abortion, she had confronted him on this, finally he did pay part of the money); this second football player and the woman began to quarrel and he threatened that, unless she submit to him sexually, he would throw her out the third-story window; then he raped her; four other football players also raped her; during the gang rape, several other football players were in and out of the room; when the woman finally was able to leave the dormitory she drove immediately to a hospital.

Both the police investigator on the case and a source in the prosecutor's office believe the victim's story—that there was a gang rape perpetrated on her by the six Notre Dame football players.

All of the male university authorities who investigated the alleged gang rape determined that the victim was a slut. This they did, all of them, by interviewing the accused rapists. In fact, the prosecutor's character investigation indicated that the woman was a fine person. The coach of the Notre Dame football team placed responsibility for the alleged gang rape on the worsening morals of women who watch soap operas. Hesburgh, moral exemplar that he is, concluded: "I didn't need to talk to the girl. I talked to the boys." The Dean of Students, John Macheca, expelled the students as a result of his secret investigation. Hesburgh overruled the expulsion out of what he called "compassion"—he reduced the expulsion to one year's suspension. The rape victim now attends a university in the Midwest. Her life, according to Anson, has been threatened.

The fact is, as these two stories demonstrate conclusively, that any woman can be raped by any group of men. Her word will not be credible against their collective testimony. A proper investigation will not be done. Remember the good Father Hesburgh's words as long as you live: "I didn't need to talk to the girl. I talked to the boys." Even when a prosecutor is convinced that rape as defined by male law did take place, the rapists will not be prosecuted. Male university officials will protect those sacrosanct male institutions—the football team and the fraternity—no matter what the cost to women.

The reasons for this are terrible and cruel, but you must know them. Men are a privileged gender class over and against women. One of their privileges is the right of rape—that is, the right of carnal access to any woman. Men agree, by law, custom, and habit, that women are sluts and liars. Men will form alliances, or bonds, to protect their gender class interests. Even in a racist society, male bonding takes precedence over racial bonding.

It is very difficult whenever racist and sexist pathologies coincide to delineate in a political way what has actually happened. In 1838, Angelina Grimké, abolitionist and feminist, described Amerikan institutions as "a system of complicated crimes, built up upon the broken hearts and prostrate bodies of my countrymen in chains, and cemented by the blood, sweat, and tears of my sisters in bonds."[37] Racism and sexism are the warp and woof of this Amerikan society, the very fabric of our institutions, laws, customs, and habits—and we are the inheritors of that complicated system of crimes. In the Notre Dame case, for instance, we can postulate that the prosecutor took the woman's charges of rape seriously at all because her accused rapists were black. That is racism and that is sexism. There is no doubt at all that white male law is more amenable to the prosecution of blacks for the raping of white women than the other way around. We can also postulate that, had the Notre Dame case been taken to court, the rape victim's character would have been impugned irrevocably because her lover was a black. That is racism and that is sexism. We also know that had a black woman been raped, either by blacks or whites, her rape would go unprosecuted, unremarked. That is racism and that is sexism.

In general, we can observe that the lives of rapists are worth more than the lives of women who are raped. Rapists are protected by male law and rape victims are punished by male law. An intricate system of male bonding supports the right of the rapist to rape, while diminishing the worth of the victim's life to absolute zero. In the Notre Dame case, the woman's lover allowed his fellows to rape her. This was a male bond. In the course of the rape, at one point when the woman was left alone—there is no indication that she was even conscious at this point—a white football player entered the room and asked her if she wanted to leave. When she did not answer, he left her there without reporting the incident. This was a male bond. The cover-up and lack of substantive investigation by white authorities was male bonding. All women of all races should recognize that male bonding takes precedence over racial bonding except in one particular kind of rape: that is, where the woman is viewed as the property of one race, class, or nationality, and her rape is viewed as an act of aggression against the males of that race, class, or nationality. Eldridge Cleaver in *Soul on Ice* has described this sort of rape:

> I became a rapist. To refine my technique and modus operandi I started out by practicing on black girls in the ghetto . . . and when I considered myself smooth enough, I crossed the tracks and sought out white prey. I did this consciously, deliberately, willfully, methodically . . .
>
> Rape was an insurrectionary act. It delighted me that I was defying and trampling upon the white man's law, upon his system of values, and that I was defiling his women—and this point, I believe, was the most satisfying to me because I was very resentful over the historical fact of how the white man has used the black woman. I felt I was getting revenge.[38]

In this sort of rape, women are viewed as the property of men who are, by virtue of race or class or nationality, enemies. Women are viewed as the chattel of enemy men. In this situation, and in this situation only, bonds of race or class or nationality will take priority over male bonding. As Cleaver's testimony makes clear, the women of one's own group are also viewed as chattel, property, to be used at will for one's own purposes. When a black man rapes a black woman, no act of aggression against a white male has been committed, and so the man's right to rape will be defended. It is very important to remember that most rape is intraracial—that is, black men rape black women and white men rape white women—because rape is a *sexist* crime. Men rape the women they have access to as a function of their masculinity and as a signet of their ownership. Cleaver's outrage "at the historical fact of how the white man has used the black woman" is wrath over the theft of property which is rightly his. Similarly, classic Southern rage at blacks who sleep with white women is wrath over the theft of property which rightly belongs to the white male. In the Notre Dame case, we can say that the gender class interests of men were served by determining that the value of the black football players to masculine pride—that is, to the championship Notre Dame football team—took priority over the white father's very compromised claim to ownership of his daughter. The issue was *never* whether a crime had been committed against a particular woman.

Now, I have laid out the dimensions of the rape atrocity. As women, we live in the midst of a society that regards us as contemptible. We are despised, as a gender class, as sluts and liars. We are the victims of continuous, malevolent, and sanctioned violence against us—against our bodies and our whole lives. Our characters are defamed, as a gender class, so that no individual woman has any credibility before the law or in society at large. Our enemies—rapists and their defenders—not only go unpunished; they remain influential arbiters of morality; they have high and esteemed places in the society; they are priests, lawyers, judges, lawmakers, politicians, doctors, artists, corporation executives, psychiatrists, and teachers.

The Rape Atrocity and the Boy Next Door

What can we, who are powerless by definition and in fact, do about it?

First, we must effectively organize to treat the symptoms of this dread and epidemic disease. Rape crisis centers are crucial. Training in self-defense is crucial. Squads of women police formed to handle all rape cases are crucial. Women prosecutors on rape cases are crucial.

New rape laws are needed. These new laws must: (1) eliminate corroboration as a requirement for conviction; (2) eliminate the need for a rape victim to be physically injured to prove rape; (3) eliminate the need to prove lack of consent; (4) redefine *consent* to denote "meaningful and knowledgeable assent, not mere acquiescence"; (5) lower the unrealistic age of consent; (6) eliminate as admissible evidence the victim's prior sexual activity or previous consensual sex with the defendant; (7) assure that marital relationship between parties is no defense or bar to prosecution; (8) define rape in terms of degrees of serious injury.[39] These changes in the rape law were proposed by the New York University Law Clinical Program in Women's Legal Rights, and you can find their whole proposed model rape law in a book called *Rape: The First Sourcebook for Women*, by the New York Radical Feminists. I recommend to you that you investigate this proposal and then work for its implementation.

Also, we must, in order to protect ourselves, refuse to participate in the dating system which sets up every woman as a potential rape victim. In the dating system, women are defined as the passive pleasers of any and every man. The worth of any woman is measured by her ability to attract and please men. The object of the dating game for the man is "to score." In playing this game, as women we put ourselves and our well-being in the hands of virtual or actual strangers. As women, we must analyze this dating system to determine its explicit and implicit definitions and values. In analyzing it, we will see how we are coerced into becoming sex-commodities.

Also, we must actively seek to publicize unprosecuted cases

of rape, and we must make the identities of rapists known to other women.

There is also work here for men who do not endorse the right of men to rape. In Philadelphia, men have formed a group called Men Organized Against Rape. They deal with male relatives and friends of rape victims in order to dispel belief in the myth of female culpability. Sometimes rapists who are troubled by their continued aggression against women will call and ask for help. There are vast educative and counseling possibilities here. Also, in Lorton, Virginia, convicted sex offenders have organized a group called Prisoners Against Rape. They work with feminist task forces and individuals to delineate rape as a political crime against women and to find strategies for combating it. It is very important that men who want to work against rape do not, through ignorance, carelessness, or malice, reinforce sexist attitudes. Statements such as "Rape is a crime against men too" or "Men are also victims of rape" do more harm than good. It is a bitter truth that rape becomes a visible crime only when a man is forcibly sodomized. It is a bitter truth that men's sympathy can be roused when rape is viewed as "a crime against men too." These truths are too bitter for us to bear. Men who want to work against rape will have to cultivate a rigorous antisexist consciousness and discipline so that they will not, in fact, make us invisible victims once again.

It is the belief of many men that their sexism is manifested only in relation to women—that is, that if they refrain from blatantly chauvinistic behavior in the presence of women, then they are not implicated in crimes against women. That is not so. It is in male bonding that men most often jeopardize the lives of women. It is among men that men do the most to contribute to crimes against women. For instance, it is the habit and custom of men to discuss with each other their sexual intimacies with particular women in vivid and graphic terms. This kind of bonding sets up a particular woman as the rightful and inevitable sexual conquest of a man's male friends and leads to innumerable cases of rape. Women are raped often by the male friends of their male friends. Men should understand that they jeopardize women's lives by participating in the rituals of privileged boyhood. Rape is also effectively sanctioned by men who harass women on the streets and in other public places; who describe or refer to women in objectifying, demeaning ways; who act aggressively or contemptuously toward women; who tell or laugh at misogynistic jokes; who write stories or make movies where women are raped and love it; who consume or endorse pornography; who insult specific women or women as a group; who impede or ridicule women in our struggle for dignity. Men who do or who endorse these behaviors are the enemies of women and are implicated in the crime of rape. Men who want to support women in our struggle for freedom and justice should understand that it is not terrifically important to us that they learn to cry; it is important to us that they stop the crimes of violence against us.

I have been describing, of course, emergency measures, designed to help women survive as atrocity is being waged against us. How can we end the atrocity itself? Clearly, we must determine the root causes of rape and we must work to excise from our social fabric all definitions, values, and behaviors which energize and sanction rape.

What, then, are the root causes of rape?

Rape is the direct consequence of our polar definitions of men and women. Rape is *congruent* with these definitions; rape *inheres* in these definitions. Remember, rape is not committed by psychopaths or deviants from our social norms—rape is committed by *exemplars* of our social norms. In this male-supremacist society, men are defined as one order of being over and against women who are defined as another, opposite, entirely different order of being. Men are defined as aggressive, dominant, powerful. Women are defined as passive, submissive, powerless. Given these polar gender definitions, it is the very nature of men to aggress sexually against women. Rape occurs when a man, who is dominant by definition, takes a woman who, according to men and all the organs of their culture, was put on this earth for his use and gratification. Rape, then, is the logical consequence of a system of definitions of what is normative. Rape is no excess, no aberration, no accident, no mistake—it embodies sexuality as the culture defines it. As long as these definitions remain intact— that is, as long as men are defined as sexual aggressors and women are defined as passive receptors lacking integrity— men who are exemplars of the norm will rape women.

In this society, the norm of masculinity is phallic aggression. Male sexuality is, by definition, intensely and rigidly phallic. A man's identity is located in his conception of himself as the possessor of a phallus; a man's worth is located in his *pride* in phallic identity. The main characteristic of phallic identity is that *worth* is entirely contingent on the possession of a phallus. Since men have no other criteria for worth, no other notion of identity, those who do not have phalluses are not recognized as fully human.

In thinking about this, you must realize that this is not a question of heterosexual or homosexual. Male homosexuality is not a renunciation of phallic identity. Heterosexual and homosexual men are equally invested in phallic identity. They manifest this investment differently in one area—the choice of what men call a "sexual object"—but their common valuation of women consistently reinforces their own sense of phallic worth.

It is this phallocentric identity of men that makes it possible —indeed, necessary—for men to view women as a lower order of creation. Men genuinely do not know that women are individual persons of worth, volition, and sensibility because *masculinity* is the signet of all worth, and masculinity is a function of phallic identity. Women, then, by definition, have no claim to the rights and responsibilities of personhood. Wonderful George Gilder, who can always be counted on to tell us the dismal truth about masculinity, has put it this way: ". . . unlike femininity, relaxed masculinity is at bottom empty, a limp nullity. . . . Manhood at the most basic level can be validated and expressed only in action."[40] And so, what are the actions that validate and express this masculinity: rape, first and foremost rape; murder, war, plunder, fighting, imperializing and colonializing—*aggression* in any and every form, and to any and every degree. All personal, psychological, social, and institutionalized domination on this earth can be traced back to its source: the phallic identities of men.

As women, of course, we do not have phallic identities, and so we are defined as opposite from and inferior to men. Men consider physical strength, for instance, to be implicit in and derived from phallic identity, and so for thousands of years we have been systematically robbed of our physical strength. Men consider intellectual accomplishment to be a function of phallic identity, and so we are intellectually incompetent by their definition. Men consider moral acuity to be a function of phallic identity, and so we are consistently characterized as vain, malicious, and immoral creatures. Even the notion that women need to be fucked—which is the *a priori* assumption of the rapist—is directly derived from the specious conviction that the only worth is phallic worth: men are willing, or able, to recognize us only when we have attached to us a cock in the course of sexual intercourse. Then, and only then, we are for them *real women*.

As nonphallic beings, women are defined as submissive, passive, virtually inert. For all of patriarchal history, we have been defined by law, custom, and habit as inferior because of our nonphallic bodies. Our sexual definition is one of "masochistic passivity": "masochistic" because even men recognize their systematic sadism against us; "passivity" not because we are naturally passive, but because our chains are very heavy and as a result, we cannot move.

The fact is that in order to stop rape, and all of the other systematic abuses against us, we must destroy these very definitions of masculinity and femininity, of men and women. We must destroy completely and for all time the personality structures "dominant-active, or male" and "submissive-passive, or female." We must excise them from our social fabric, destroy any and all institutions based on them, render them vestigial, useless. We must destroy the very structure of culture as we know it, its art, its churches, its laws; we must eradicate from consciousness and memory all of the images, institutions, and structural mental sets that turn men into rapists by definition and women into victims by definition. Until we do, rape will remain our primary sexual model and women will be raped by men.

As women, we must begin this revolutionary work. When we change, those who define themselves over and against us will have to kill us all, change, or die. In order to change, we must renounce every male definition we have ever learned; we must renounce male definitions and descriptions of our lives, our bodies, our needs, our wants, our worth—we must take for ourselves the power of naming. We must refuse to be complicit in a sexual-social system that is built on our labor as an inferior slave class. We must unlearn the passivity we have been trained to over thousands of years. We must unlearn the masochism we have been trained to over thousands of years. And, most importantly, in freeing ourselves, we must refuse to imitate the phallic identities of men. We must not internalize their values and we must not replicate their crimes.

In 1870, Susan B. Anthony wrote to a friend:

> So while I do not pray for anybody or any party to commit outrages, still I do pray, and that earnestly and constantly, for some terrific shock to startle the women of this nation into a self-respect which will compel them to see the abject degradation of their present position; which will force them to break their yoke of bondage, and give them faith in themselves; which will make them proclaim their allegiance to woman first; which will enable them to see that man can no more feel, speak, or act for woman than could the old slaveholder for his slave. The fact is, women

5

The Sexual Politics of Fear and Courage

(For my mother)

(1)

I want to talk to you about fear and courage—what each is, how they are related to each other, and what place each has in a woman's life.

When I was trying to think through what to say here today, I thought that I might just tell stories—stories of the lives of very brave women. There are many such stories to tell, and I am always inspired by these stories, and I thought that you might be too. But, while these stories always enable us to feel a kind of collective pride, they also allow us to mystify particular acts of courage and to deify those who have committed them—we say, oh, yes, she was like that, but I am not; we say, she was such an extraordinary woman, but I am not. So I

Delivered at Queens College, City University of New York, March 12, 1975; Fordham University, New York City, December 16, 1975.

are in chains, and their servitude is all the more debasing because they do not realize it. O, to compel them to see and feel, and to give them the courage and conscience to speak and act for their own freedom, though they face the scorn and contempt of all the world for doing it.[41]

Isn't rape the outrage that will do this, sisters, and isn't it time?

decided to try to think through fear and courage in another way—in a more analytical, political way.

I am going to try to delineate for you the sexual politics of fear and courage—that is, how fear is learned as a function of femininity; and how courage is the red badge of masculinity.

I believe that we are all products of the culture in which we live; and that in order to understand what we think of as our personal experiences, we must understand *first* how the culture informs what we see and how we understand. In other words, the culture in which we live determines for us to an astonishing degree how we perceive, what we perceive, how we name and value our experiences, how and why we act at all.

The first fact of this culture is that it is *male supremacist*: that is, men are, by birthright, law, custom, and habit, systematically and consistently defined as superior to women. This definition, which postulates that men are a gender class over and against women, inheres in every organ and institution of this culture. There are no exceptions to this particular rule.

In a male supremacist culture, the *male condition* is taken to be the human condition, so that, when any man speaks—for instance, as an artist, historian, or philosopher—he speaks *objectively*—that is, as someone who has, by definition, no special bone to pick, no special investment which would slant his view; he is somehow an embodiment of the norm. Women, on the other hand, are not men. Therefore women are, by virtue of male logic, not the norm, a different, lower order of being, subjective rather than objective, a confused amalgam of special bones to pick which make our perceptions, judgments, and decisions untrustworthy, not credible, whimsical. Simone de Beauvoir in the preface to *The Second Sex* described it this way:

> In actuality the relation of the two sexes is not . . . like that of two electrical poles, for man represents both the positive and the neutral, as is indicated by the common use of *man* to designate

human beings in general; whereas woman represents only the negative, defined by limiting criteria, without reciprocity. . . . "The female is a female by virtue of a certain *lack* of qualities," said Aristotle; "we should regard the female nature as afflicted with a natural defectiveness." And St. Thomas for his part pronounced woman to be an "imperfect man," an "incidental" being...

Thus, humanity is male and man defines woman not in herself but as relative to him; she is not regarded as an autonomous being.[1]

We can locate easily the precise way in which we are "afflicted with a natural defectiveness." As Freud so eloquently put it two millennia after Aristotle:

[Women] notice the penis of a brother or playmate, strikingly visible and of large proportions, [and] at once recognize it as the superior counterpart of their own small and inconspicuous organ. . . .

. . . After a woman has become aware of the wound to her narcissism, she develops, like a scar, a sense of inferiority. When she has passed beyond her first attempt at explaining her lack of a penis as being a punishment personal to herself and has realized that that sexual character is a universal one, she begins to share the contempt felt by men for a sex which is the lesser in so important a respect . . . [2]

Now, the terrible truth is that in a patriarchy, possession of a phallus is the sole signet of worth, the touchstone of *human* identity. All positive human attributes are seen as inherent in and consequences of that single biological accident. Intellect, moral discernment, creativity, imagination—all are male, or phallic, faculties. When any woman develops any one of these faculties, we are told either that she is striving to behave "like a man" or that she is "masculine."

One particularly important attribute of phallic identity is courage. Manhood can be functionally described as the capacity for courageous action. A man is *born* with that capacity—

that is, with a phallus. Each tiny male infant is a potential hero. His mother is supposed to raise and nurture him so that he can develop that inherent capacity. His father is supposed to embody in the world that capacity fully realized.

Any work or activity that a male does, or any nascent talent that a male might have, has a mythic dimension: it can be recognized by male culture as heroic and the manhood of any male who embodies it is thereby affirmed.

The kinds and categories of mythic male heroes are numerous. A man can be a hero if he climbs a mountain, or plays football, or pilots an airplane. A man can be a hero if he writes a book, or composes a piece of music, or directs a play. A man can be a hero if he is a scientist, or a soldier, or a drug addict, or a disc jockey, or a crummy mediocre politician. A man can be a hero because he suffers and despairs; or because he thinks logically and analytically; or because he is "sensitive"; or because he is cruel. Wealth establishes a man as a hero, and so does poverty. Virtually any circumstance in a man's life will make him a hero to some group of people and has a mythic rendering in the culture—in literature, art, theater, or the daily newspapers.

It is precisely this mythic dimension of all male activity which reifies the gender class system so that male supremacy is unchallengeable and unchangeable. Women are never confirmed as heroic or courageous agents because the capacity for courageous action inheres in maleness itself—it is identifiable and affirmable only as a male capacity. Women, remember, are "female by virtue of a certain *lack* of qualities." One of the qualities we must lack in order to pass as female is the capacity for courageous action.

This goes right to the core of female invisibility in this culture. No matter what we do, we are not seen. Our acts are not witnessed, not observed, not experienced, not recorded, not affirmed. Our acts have no mythic dimension in male terms simply because we are not men, we do not have phalluses. When men do not see a cock, they do not in fact see anything;

they perceive a *lack* of qualities, an absence. They see nothing of value since they only recognize phallic value; and they cannot value what they do not see. They may fill in the empty spaces, the absence, with all sorts of monstrous imaginings—for instance, they may imagine that the vagina is a hole filled with teeth—but they cannot recognize a woman for who she is as a discrete, actual being; nor can they grasp what a woman's body is to her, that is, that she experiences herself as actual, and not as the negative of a man; nor can they understand that women are not "empty" inside. This last male illusion, or hallucination, is as interesting as it is shocking. I have often heard men describe the vagina as "empty space"—the notion being that the defining characteristic of women from the top of the legs to the waist is internal emptiness. Somehow, the illusion is that women contain an internal space which is an absence and which must be filled—either by a phallus or by a child, which is viewed as an extension of the phallus. Erik Erikson's rendition of this male fantasy sanctified it for psychologists. Erikson wrote:

> No doubt also, the very existence of the inner productive space exposes women early to a specific sense of loneliness, to a fear of being left empty or deprived of treasures, of remaining unfulfilled and of drying up . . . in female experience an "inner space" is at the center of despair even as it is the very center of potential fulfillment. Emptiness is the female form of perdition . . . [it is] standard experience for all women. To be left, for her, means to be left empty . . . Such hurt can be re-experienced in each menstruation; it is a crying to heaven in the mourning over a child; and it becomes a permanent scar in the menopause.[3]

It is no wonder, then, that men recognize us only when we have a phallus attached to us in the course of sexual intercourse or when we are pregnant. Then we are for them *real women*; then we have, in their eyes, an identity, a function, a verifiable existence; then, and only then, we are not "empty." The isolation of this male pathology, by the way, sheds some light on the abortion struggle. In a society in which the only recognizable worth is phallic worth, it is unconscionable for a woman to choose to "be empty inside," to choose to be "deprived of treasures." The womb is dignified only when it is the repository of holy goods—the phallus or, since men want sons, the fetal son. To abort a fetus, in masculinist terms, is to commit an act of violence against the phallus itself. It is akin to chopping off a cock. Because a fetus is perceived of as having a phallic character, its so-called life is valued very highly, while the woman's actual life is worthless and invisible since she can make no claim to phallic potentiality.

It may sound peculiar, at first, to speak of fear as the absence of courage. We know, all of us, that fear is vivid, actual, physiologically verifiable—but then, so is the vagina. We live in a male-imagined world, and our lives are circumscribed by the limits of male imagination. Those limits are very severe.

As women, we learn fear as a function of our so-called femininity. We are taught systematically to be afraid, and we are taught that to be afraid not only is congruent with femininity, but also inheres in it. We are taught to be afraid so that we will not be able to act, so that we will be passive, so that we will be women—so that we will be, as Aristotle put it so charmingly, "afflicted with a natural defectiveness."

In *Woman Hating*, I described how this process is embodied in the fairy tales we all learn as children:

> The lessons are simple, and we learn them well.
>
> Men and women are different, absolute opposites.
>
> The heroic prince can never be confused with Cinderella, or Snow-white, or Sleeping Beauty. She could never do what he does at all, let alone better. . . .
>
> Where he is erect, she is supine. Where he is awake, she is asleep. Where he is active, she is passive. Where she is erect, or awake, or active, she is evil and must be destroyed. . . .
>
> There are two definitions of woman. There is the good woman. She is a victim. There is the bad woman. She must be destroyed. The good woman must be possessed. The bad woman must be killed, or punished. Both must be nullified.

> . . . There is the good woman. She is the victim. The posture of victimization, the passivity of the victim demands abuse.
> Women strive for passivity, because women want to be good. The abuse evoked by that passivity convinces women that they are bad. . . .
> Even a woman who strives conscientiously for passivity sometimes does something. That she acts at all provokes abuse. The abuse provoked by that activity convinces her that she is bad. . . .
> The moral of the story should, one would think, preclude a happy ending. It does not. The moral of the story is the happy ending. It tells us that happiness for a woman is to be passive, victimized, destroyed, or asleep. It tells us that happiness is for the woman who is good—inert, passive, victimized—and that a good woman is a happy woman. It tells us that the happy ending is when we are ended, when we live without our lives or not at all.[4]

Every organ of this male supremacist culture embodies the complex and odious system of rewards and punishments which will teach a woman her proper place, her allowable sphere. Family, school, church; books, movies, television; games, songs, toys—all teach a girl to submit and conform long before she becomes a woman.

The fact is that a girl is forced, through an effective and pervasive system of rewards and punishments, to develop precisely the *lack* of qualities which will certify her as a woman. In developing this lack of qualities, she is forced to learn to punish herself for any violation of the rules of behavior that apply to her gender class. Her arguments with the very definitions of womanhood are internalized so that, in the end, she argues against herself—against the validity of any impulse toward action or assertion; against the validity of any claim to self-respect and dignity; against the validity of any ambition to accomplishment or excellence outside her allowable sphere. She polices and punishes herself; but should this internal value system break down for any reason, there is always a psychiatrist, professor, minister, lover, father, or son around to force her back into the feminine flock.

Now, you all know that other women will also act as agents

of this mammoth repression. It is the first duty of mothers under patriarchy to cultivate heroic sons and to make their daughters willing to accommodate themselves to what has been accurately described as a "half-life." All women are supposed to vilify any peer who deviates from the accepted norm of femininity, and most do. What is remarkable is not that most do, but that some do not.

The position of the mother, in particular, in a male supremacist society, is absolutely untenable. Freud, in yet another astonishing insight, asserted, "A mother is only brought unlimited satisfaction by her relation to a son; this is altogether the most perfect, the most free from ambivalence of all human relationships."[5] The fact is that it is easier for a woman to raise a son than a daughter. First, she is rewarded for bearing a son—this is the pinnacle of possible accomplishment for her in her life, as viewed by male culture. We might say that in bearing a son, she has had a phallus inside her empty space for nine months, and that that assures her of approval which she could not earn in any other way. She is then expected to invest the rest of her life in maintaining, nourishing, nurturing, and hallowing that son. But the fact is that that son has a birthright to identity which she is denied. He has a right to embody actual qualities, to develop talents, to act, to become—to become who or what she could not become. It is impossible to imagine that this relationship is not saturated with ambivalence for the mother, with ambivalence and with downright bitterness. This ambivalence, this bitterness, is intrinsic to the mother-son relationship because the son will inevitably betray the mother by becoming a man —that is, by accepting his birthright to power over and against her and her kind.[6] But for a mother the *project* of raising a boy is the most fulfilling project she can hope for. She can watch him, as a child, play the games she was not allowed to play; she can invest in him her ideas, aspirations, ambitions, and values—or whatever she has left of them; she can watch her son, who came from her flesh and whose life was sustained by her work and devotion, embody her in the world. So while the project of raising a boy is fraught with ambivalence and leads inevitably to bitterness, it is the only project that allows a woman *to be*—to be *through* her son, to live through her son.

The project of raising a girl, on the other hand, is torturous. The mother must succeed in teaching her daughter *not to be*; she must force her daughter into developing the lack of qualities that will enable her to pass as female. The mother is the primary agent of male culture in the family, and she must force her daughter to acquiesce to the demands of that culture.[7] She must do to her daughter what was done to her. The fact that we are all trained to be mothers from infancy on means that we are all trained to devote our lives to men, whether they are our sons or not; that we are all trained to force other women to exemplify the lack of qualities which characterizes the cultural construct of femininity.

Fear cements this system together. Fear is the adhesive that holds each part in its place. We learn to be afraid of the punishment which is inevitable when we violate the code of enforced femininity.

We learn that certain fears are in and of themselves feminine—for instance, girls are supposed to be afraid of bugs and mice. As children, we are rewarded for learning these fears. Girls are taught to be afraid of all activities which are expressly designated as male terrain—running, climbing, playing ball; mathematics and science; composing music, earning money, providing leadership. Any list could go on and on— because the fact is that girls are taught to be afraid of everything except domestic work and childrearing. By the time we are women, fear is as familiar to us as air. It is our element. We live in it, we inhale it, we exhale it, and most of the time we do not even notice it. Instead of "I am afraid," we say, "I don't want to," or "I don't know how," or "I can't."

Fear, then, is a learned response. It is not a human instinct which manifests itself differently in women and in men. The whole question of instinct versus learned response in human beings is a specious one. As Evelyn Reed says in her book, *Woman's Evolution*:

> The essence of socializing the animal is to break the absolute dictation of nature and replace purely animal instincts with conditioned responses and learned behavior. Humans today have shed their original animal instincts to such a degree that most have vanished. A child, for example, must be taught the dangers of fire, which animals flee instinctively.[8]

We are separated from our instincts, whatever they were, by thousands of years of patriarchal culture. What we know and what we act on is what we have been taught. Women have been taught fear as a function of femininity, just as men have been taught courage as a function of masculinity.

What is fear then? What are its characteristics? What is it about fear that is so effective in compelling women to be good soldiers on the side of the enemy?

Fear, as women experience it, has three main characteristics: it is isolating; it is confusing; and it is debilitating.

When a woman violates a rule which spells out her proper behavior as a female, she is singled out by men, their agents, and their culture as a troublemaker. The rebel's isolation is real in that she is avoided, or ignored, or chastised, or denounced. Acceptance back into the community of men, which is the only viable and sanctioned community, is contingent on her renunciation and repudiation of her deviant behavior.

Every girl as she is growing up experiences this form and fact of isolation. She learns that it is an inevitable consequence of any rebellion, however small. By the time she is a woman, fear and isolation are tangled into a hard, internal knot so that she cannot experience one without the other. The terror which plagues women at even the thought of being "alone" in life is directly derived from this conditioning. If there is a form of "female perdition" under patriarchy, surely it is this dread of isolation—a dread which develops from the facts of the case.

Confusion, too, is an integral part of fear. It is confusing to be punished for succeeding—for climbing a tree, or excelling in mathematics. It is impossible to answer the question, "What did I do wrong?" As a result of the punishment which is inevitable when she succeeds, a girl learns to identify fear with confusion and confusion with fear. By the time she is a woman, fear and confusion are triggered simultaneously by the same stimuli and they cannot be separated from each other.

Fear, for women, is isolating and confusing. It is also consistently and progressively debilitating. Each act outside a woman's allowable sphere provokes punishment—and this punishment is as inevitable as nightfall. Each punishment inculcates fear. Like a rat, a woman will try to avoid those high-voltage electric shocks which seem to mine the maze. She too wants the legendary Big Cheese at the end. But for her, the maze never ends.

The debility which is intrinsic to fear as women experience it is progressive. It increases not arithmetically as she gets older, but geometrically. The first time a girl breaks a gender class rule and is punished, she has only the actual consequences of her act with which to contend. That is, she is isolated, confused, and afraid. But the second time, she must contend with her act, its consequences, *and also* with her memory of a prior act and its prior consequences. This interplay of the memory of pain, the anticipation of pain, and the reality of pain in a given circumstance makes it virtually impossible for a woman to perceive the daily indignities to which she is subjected, much less to assert herself against them or to develop and stand for values which undermine or oppose male supremacy. The effects of this cumulative, progressive, debilitating aspect of fear are mutilating, and male culture provides only one possible resolution: complete and abject submission.

This dynamic of fear, as I have described it, is the source of what men so glibly, and happily, call "female masochism."

And, of course, when one's identity is defined as a lack of identity; when one's survival is contingent on learning to destroy or restrain every impulse toward self-definition; when one is consistently and exclusively rewarded for hurting oneself by conforming to demeaning or degrading rules of behavior; when one is consistently and inevitably punished for accomplishing, or succeeding, or asserting; when one is battered and rammed, physically and/or emotionally, for any act or thought of rebellion, and then applauded and approved of for giving in, recanting, apologizing; then masochism does indeed become the cornerstone of one's personality. And, as you might already know, it is very hard for masochists to find the pride, the strength, the inner freedom, the *courage* to organize against their oppressors.

The truth is that this masochism, which does become the core of the female personality, is the mechanism which assures that the system of male supremacy will continue to operate as a whole even if parts of the system itself break down or are reformed. For example, if the male supremacist system is reformed, so that the law requires that there be no discrimination in employment on the basis of gender and that there be equal pay for equal work, the masochistic conditioning of women will cause us to continue, despite the change in law, to replicate the patterns of female inferiority which consign us to menial jobs appropriate to our gender class. This dynamic insures that no series of economic or legal reforms will end male domination. The internal mechanism of female masochism must be rooted out from the inside before women will ever know what it is to be free.

(2)

Now, the feminist project is to end male domination—to obliterate it from the face of this earth. We also want to end those forms of social injustice which derive from the patriarchal model of male dominance—that is, imperialism, colonialism, racism, war, poverty, violence in every form.

In order to do this, we will have to destroy the structure of culture as we know it, its art, its churches, its laws; its nuclear families based on father-right and nation-states; all of the images, institutions, customs, and habits which define women as worthless and invisible victims.

In order to destroy the structure of patriarchal culture, we will have to destroy male and female sexual identities as we now know them—in other words, we will have to abandon phallic worth and female masochism altogether as normative, sanctioned identities, as modes of erotic behavior, as basic indicators of "male" and "female."

As we are destroying the structure of culture, we will have to build a new culture—nonhierarchical, nonsexist, noncoercive, nonexploitative—in other words, a culture which is not based on dominance and submission in any way.

As we are destroying the phallic identities of men and the masochistic identities of women, we will have to create, out of our own ashes, new erotic identities. These new erotic identities will have to repudiate at their core the male sexual model: that is, they will have to repudiate the personality structures dominant-active ("male") and submissive-passive ("female"); they will have to repudiate genital sexuality as the primary focus and value of erotic identity; they will have to repudiate and obviate all of the forms of erotic objectification and alienation which inhere in the male sexual model.[9]

How can we, women, who have been taught to be afraid of every little noise in the night, dare to imagine that we might destroy the world that men defend with their armies and their lives? How can we, women, who have no vivid memory of ourselves as heroes, imagine that we might succeed in building a revolutionary community? Where can we find the revolutionary courage to overcome our slave fear?

Sadly, we are as invisible to ourselves as we are to men. We learn to see with their eyes—and they are near blind. Our first task, as feminists, is to learn to see with our own eyes.

If we could see with our own eyes, I believe that we would

see that we already have, in embryonic form, the qualities required to overturn the male supremacist system which oppresses us and which threatens to destroy all life on this planet. We would see that we already have, in embryonic form, values on which to build a new world. We would see that female strength and courage have developed out of the very circumstances of our oppression, out of our lives as breeders and domestic chattel. Until now, we have used those qualities to endure under devastating and terrifying conditions. Now we must use those qualities of female strength and courage which developed in us as mothers and wives to repudiate the very slave conditions from which they are derived.

If we were not invisible to ourselves, we would see that since the beginning of time, we have been the exemplars of physical courage. Squatting in fields, isolated in bedrooms, in slums, in shacks, or in hospitals, women endure the ordeal of giving birth. This physical act of giving birth requires physical courage of the highest order. It is the prototypical act of authentic physical courage. One's life is each time on the line. One faces death each time. One endures, withstands, or is consumed by pain. Survival demands stamina, strength, concentration, and will power. No phallic hero, no matter what he does to himself or to another to prove his courage, ever matches the solitary, existential courage of the woman who gives birth.

We need not continue to have children in order to claim the dignity of realizing our own capacity for physical courage. This capacity is ours; it belongs to us, and it has belonged to us since the beginning of time. What we must do now is to reclaim this capacity—take it out of the service of men; make it visible to ourselves; and determine how to use it in the service of feminist revolution.

If we were not invisible to ourselves, we would also see that we have always had a resolute commitment to and faith in human life which have made us heroic in our nurturance and sustenance of lives other than our own. Under all circumstances—in war, sickness, famine, drought, poverty, in times of incalculable misery and despair—women have done the work required for the survival of the species. We have not pushed a button, or organized a military unit, to do the work of emotionally and physically sustaining life. We have done it one by one, and one to one. For thousands of years, in my view, women have been the only exemplars of moral and spiritual courage—we have sustained life, while men have taken it. This capacity for sustaining life belongs to us. We must reclaim it—take it out of the service of men, so that it will never again be used by them in their own criminal interests.

Also, if we were not invisible to ourselves, we would see that most women can bear, and have for centuries borne, any anguish—physical or mental—for the sake of those they love. It is time to reclaim this kind of courage too, and to use it for ourselves and each other.

For us, historically, courage has always been a function of our resolute commitment to life. Courage as we know it has developed from that commitment. We have always faced death for the sake of life; and even in the bitterness of our domestic slavery, we were sustained by the knowledge that we were ourselves sustaining life.

We are faced, then, with two facts of female existence under patriarchy: (1) that we are taught fear as a function of femininity; and (2) that under the very slave conditions which we must repudiate, we have developed a heroic commitment to sustaining and nurturing life.

In our lifetimes, we will not be able to eradicate that first fact of female existence under patriarchy: we will continue to be afraid of the punishments which are inevitable as we challenge male supremacy; we will find it hard to root out the masochism which is so deeply embedded within us; we will suffer ambivalence and conflict, most of us, throughout our lives as we advance our revolutionary feminist presence.

But, if we are resolute, we will also deepen and expand that heroic commitment to sustaining and nurturing life. We will deepen it by creating visionary new forms of human community; we will expand it by including ourselves in it—by learning to value and cherish each other as sisters. We will renounce all forms of male control and male domination; we will destroy the institutions and cultural valuations which imprison us in invisibility and victimization; but we will take with us, out of our bitter, bitter past, our passionate identification with the worth of other human lives.

I want to end by saying that we must never betray the heroic commitment to the worth of human life which is the source of our courage as women. If we do betray that commitment, we will find ourselves, hands dripping with blood, equal heroes to men at last.

6

Redefining Nonviolence

> ... and finally I twist my heart round again, so that the bad is on the outside and the good is on the inside and keep on trying to find a way of becoming what I would so like to be, and I could be, if ... there weren't any other people living in the world.
> Anne Frank, *The Diary of a Young Girl*,
> August 1, 1944, three days before her arrest

(1)

Feminism, according to *The Random House Dictionary*, is defined as "the doctrine advocating social and political rights of women equal to those of men." This is one tenet of feminism, and I urge you not to sneer at it, not to deride it as reformist, not to dismiss it with what you might consider left-wing radical purity.

Some of you fought with all your heart and soul for civil rights for blacks. You understood that to sit at a dirty lunch counter and eat a rotten hamburger had no revolutionary validity at all—and yet you also understood the indignity, the demeaning indignity, of not being able to do so. And so you, and others like you, laid your lives on the line so that blacks would not be forced to suffer systematic daily indignities of exclusion from institutions which, in fact, you did not endorse. In all the

Delivered at Boston College, at a conference on Alternatives to the Military-Corporate System, in a panel on "Defending Values Without Violence," April 5, 1975.

years of the civil rights movement, I never heard a white male radical say to a black man—"Why do you want to eat there, it's so much nicer eating grits at home." It was understood that racism was a festering pathology, and that that pathology had to be challenged wherever its dread symptoms appeared: to check the growth of the pathology itself; to diminish its debilitating effects on its victims; to try to save black lives, one by one if necessary, from the ravages of a racist system which condemned those lives to a bitter misery.

And yet, when it comes to your own lives, you do not make the same claim. Sexism, which is properly defined as the systematic cultural, political, social, sexual, psychological, and economic servitude of women to men and to patriarchal institutions, is a festering pathology too. It festers in every house, on every street, in every law court, in every job situation, on every television show, in every movie. It festers in virtually every transaction between a man and a woman. It festers in every encounter between a woman and the institutions of this male-dominated society. Sexism festers when we are raped, or when we are married. It festers when we are denied absolute control over our own bodies—whenever the state or any man decides in our stead the uses to which our bodies will be put. Sexism festers when we are taught to submit to men, sexually and/or intellectually. It festers when we are taught and forced to serve men in their kitchens, in their beds, as domestics, as shit workers in their multifarious causes, as devoted disciples of their work, whatever that work may be. It festers when we are taught and forced to nourish them as wives, mothers, lovers, or daughters. Sexism festers when we are forced to study male culture but are allowed no recognition of or pride in our own. It festers when we are taught to venerate and respect male voices, so that we have no voices of our own. Sexism festers when, from infancy on, we are forced to restrain every impulse toward adventure, every ambition toward achievement or greatness, every bold or original act or idea. Sexism festers day and night, day after day, night after night. Sexism is the foundation on which all tyranny is built. Every social form of hierarchy and abuse is modeled on male-over-female domination.

I have never heard a white male radical ridicule or denigrate a black man for demanding that the Civil Rights Act be passed, or for recognizing the racist values behind any refusal to vote for that act. Yet, many left-wing women have said to me, "I can't quite figure out the politics of the Equal Rights Amendment." Further discussion always reveals that these women have been denigrated by left-wing men for being distressed that the Equal Rights Amendment might not pass this year or in the near future. Let me tell you about "the politics of the Equal Rights Amendment"—a refusal to pass it is a refusal to recognize women as being sound enough in mind and body to exercise the rights of citizenship; a refusal to pass it condemns women to lives as nonentities before the law; a refusal to pass it is an affirmation of the view that women are inferior to men by virtue of biology, as a condition of birth. Among political people, it is shameful to be a racist or an anti-Semite. No shame attaches to a resolute disregard for the civil rights of women.

In my view, any man who truly recognizes your right to dignity and to freedom will recognize that the dread symptoms of sexism must be challenged wherever they appear: to check the growth of the pathology itself; to diminish its debilitating effects on its victims; to try to save women's lives, one by one if necessary, from the ravages of a sexist system which condemns those lives to a bitter misery. Any man who is your comrade will know in his gut the indignity, the demeaning indignity, of systematic exclusion from the rights and responsibilities of citizenship. Any man who is your true comrade will be committed to laying his body, his life, on the line so that you will be subjected to that indignity no longer. I ask you to look to your male comrades on the left, and to determine whether they have made that commitment to you. If they have not, then they do not take your lives seriously, and as long as you work for and with them, you do not take your lives seriously either.

(2)

Feminism is an exploration, one that has just begun. Women have been taught that, for us, the earth is flat, and that if we venture out, we will fall off the edge. Some of us have ventured out nevertheless, and so far we have not fallen off. It is my faith, my feminist faith, that we will not.

Our exploration has three parts. First, we must discover our past. The road back is obscure, hard to find. We look for signs that tell us: women have lived here. And then we try to see what life was like for those women. It is a bitter exploration. We find that for centuries, all through recorded time, women have been violated, exploited, demeaned, systematically and unconscionably. We find that millions upon millions of women have died as the victims of organized gynocide. We find atrocity after atrocity, executed on such a vast scale that other atrocities pale by comparison. We find that gynocide takes many forms—slaughter, crippling, mutilation, slavery, rape. It is not easy for us to bear what we see.

Second, we must examine the present: how is society presently organized; how do women live now; how does it work—this global system of oppression based on gender which takes so many invisible lives; what are the sources of male dominance; how does male dominance perpetuate itself in organized violence and totalitarian institutions? This too is a bitter exploration. We see that all over the world our people, women, are in chains. These chains are psychological, social, sexual, legal, economic. These chains are heavy. These chains are locked by a systematic violence perpetrated against us by the gender class men. It is not easy for us to bear what we see. It is not easy for us to shed these chains, to find the resources to withdraw our consent from oppression. It is not easy for us to determine what forms our resistance must take.

Third, we must imagine a future in which we would be free. Only the imagining of this future can energize us so that we do not remain victims of our past and our present. Only the imagining of this future can give us the strength to repudiate our slave behavior—to identify it whenever we manifest it, and to root it out of our lives. This exploration is not bitter, but it is insanely difficult—because each time a woman does renounce slave behavior, she meets the full force and cruelty of her oppressor head on.

Politically committed women often ask the question, "How can we as women support the struggles of other people?" This question as a basis for political analysis and action replicates the very form of our oppression—it keeps us a gender class of helpmates. If we were not women—if we were male workers, or male blacks, or male anybodies—it would be enough for us to delineate the facts of our own oppression; that alone would give our struggle credibility in radical male eyes.

But we are women, and the first fact of our oppression is that we are invisible to our oppressors. The second fact of our oppression is that we have been trained—for centuries and from infancy on—to see through their eyes, and so we are invisible to ourselves. The third fact of our oppression is that our oppressors are not only male heads of state, male capitalists, male militarists—but also our fathers, sons, husbands, brothers, and lovers. No other people is so entirely captured, so entirely conquered, so destitute of any memory of freedom, so dreadfully robbed of identity and culture, so absolutely slandered as a group, so demeaned and humiliated as a function of daily life. And yet, we go on, blind, and we ask over and over again, "What can we do for them?" It is time to ask, "What must they do now for us?" That question must be the first question in any political dialogue with men.

(3)

Women, for all these patriarchal centuries, have been adamant in the defense of lives other than our own. We died in

Redefining Nonviolence

childbirth so that others might live. We sustained the lives of children, husbands, fathers, and brothers in war, in famine, in every sort of devastation. We have done this in the bitterness of global servitude. Whatever can be known under patriarchy about commitment to life, we know it. Whatever it takes to make that commitment under patriarchy, we have it.

It is time now to repudiate patriarchy by valuing our own lives as fully, as seriously, as resolutely, as we have valued other lives. It is time now to commit ourselves to the nurturance and protection of each other.

We must *establish* values which *originate* in sisterhood. We must establish values which repudiate phallic supremacy, which repudiate phallic aggression, which repudiate all relationships and institutions based on male dominance and female submission.

It will not be easy for us to establish values which originate in sisterhood. For centuries, we have had male values slammed down our throats and slammed up our cunts. We are the victims of a violence so pervasive, so constant, so relentless and unending, that we cannot point to it and say, "There it begins and there it ends." All of the values which we might defend as a consequence of our allegiances to men and their ideas are saturated with the fact or memory of that violence. We know more about violence than any other people on the face of this earth. We have absorbed such quantities of it—as women, *and* as Jews, blacks, Vietnamese, native Americans, etc.—that our bodies and souls are seared through with the effects of it.

I suggest to you that any commitment to nonviolence which is real, which is authentic, must begin in the recognition of the forms and degrees of violence perpetrated against women by the gender class men. I suggest to you that any analysis of violence, or any commitment to act against it, which does not begin there is hollow, meaningless—a sham which will have, as its direct consequence, the perpetuation of your servitude. I suggest to you that any male apostle of so-called nonviolence who is not committed, body and soul, to ending the violence against you is not trustworthy. He is not your comrade, not your brother, not your friend. He is someone to whom your life is invisible.

As women, nonviolence must begin for us in the refusal to be violated, in the refusal to be victimized. We must find alternatives to submission, because our submission—to rape, to assault, to domestic servitude, to abuse and victimization of every sort—perpetuates violence.

The refusal to be a victim does not originate in any act of resistance as male-derived as killing. The refusal of which I speak is a revolutionary refusal to be a victim, any time, any place, for friend or foe. This refusal requires the conscientious unlearning of all the forms of masochistic submission which are taught to us as the very content of womanhood. Male aggression feeds on female masochism as vultures feed on carrion. Our nonviolent project is to find the social, sexual, political, and cultural forms which repudiate our programmed submissive behaviors, so that male aggression can find no dead flesh on which to feast.

When I say that we must establish values which originate in sisterhood, I mean to say that we must not accept, even for a moment, male notions of what nonviolence is. Those notions have never condemned the systematic violence against us. The men who hold those notions have never renounced the male behaviors, privileges, values, and conceits which are in and of themselves acts of violence against us.

We will diminish violence by refusing to be violated. We will repudiate the whole patriarchal system, with its sadomasochistic institutions, with its social scenarios of dominance and submission all based on the male-over-female model, when we refuse conscientiously, rigorously, and absolutely to be the soil in which male aggression, pride, and arrogance can grow like wild weeds.

7

Lesbian Pride

For me, being a lesbian means three things—

First, it means that I love, cherish, and respect women in my mind, in my heart, and in my soul. This love of women is the soil in which my life is rooted. It is the soil of our common life together. My life grows out of this soil. In any other soil, I would die. In whatever ways I am strong, I am strong because of the power and passion of this nurturant love.

Second, being a lesbian means to me that there is an erotic passion and intimacy which comes of touch and taste, a wild, salty tenderness, a wet sweet sweat, our breasts, our mouths, our cunts, our intertangled hairs, our hands. I am speaking here of a sensual passion as deep and mysterious as the sea, as strong and still as the mountain, as insistent and changing as the wind.

Delivered at a rally for Lesbian Pride Week, Central Park, New York City, June 28, 1975.

Third, being a lesbian means to me the memory of the mother, remembered in my own body, sought for, desired, found, and truly honored. It means the memory of the womb, when we were one with our mothers, until birth when we were torn asunder. It means a return to that place inside, inside her, inside ourselves, to the tissues and membranes, to the moisture and blood.

There is a pride in the nurturant love which is our common ground, and in the sensual love, and in the memory of the mother—and that pride shines as bright as the summer sun at noon. That pride cannot be degraded. Those who would degrade it are in the position of throwing handfuls of mud at the sun. Still it shines, and those who sling mud only dirty their own hands.

Sometimes the sun is covered by dense layers of dark clouds. A person looking up would swear that there is no sun. But still the sun shines. At night, when there is no light, still the sun shines. During rain or hail or hurricane or tornado, still the sun shines.

Does the sun ask itself, "Am I good? Am I worthwhile? Is there enough of me?" No, it burns and it shines. Does the sun ask itself, "What does the moon think of me? How does Mars feel about me today?" No, it burns, it shines. Does the sun ask itself, "Am I as big as other suns in other galaxies?" No, it burns, it shines.

In this country in the coming years, I think that there will be a terrible storm. I think that the skies will darken beyond all recognition. Those who walk the streets will walk them in darkness. Those who are in prisons and mental institutions will not see the sky at all, only the dark out of barred windows. Those who are hungry and in despair may not look up at all. They will see the darkness as it lies on the ground in front of their feet. Those who are raped will see the darkness as they look up into the face of the rapist. Those who are assaulted and brutalized by madmen will stare intently into the darkness to discern who is moving toward them at every moment. It will be hard to remember, as the storm is raging, that still, even though we cannot see it, the sun shines. It will be hard to remember that still, even though we cannot see it, the sun burns. We will try to see it and we will try to feel it, and we will forget that it warms us still, that if it were not there, burning, shining, this earth would be a cold and desolate and barren place.

As long as we have life and breath, no matter how dark the earth around us, that sun still burns, still shines. There is no today without it. There is no tomorrow without it. There was no yesterday without it. That light is within us—constant, warm, and healing. Remember it, sisters, in the dark times to come.

8

Our Blood: The Slavery of Women in Amerika

(In memory of Sarah Grimké, 1792–1873, and Angelina Grimké, 1805–1879)

(1)

In her introduction to *Felix Holt* (1866), George Eliot wrote:

> ... there is much pain that is quite noiseless; and vibrations that make human agonies are often a mere whisper in the roar of hurrying existence. There are glances of hatred that stab and raise no cry of murder; robberies that leave man or woman for ever beggared of peace and joy, yet kept secret by the sufferer— committed to no sound except that of low moans in the night, seen in no writing except that made on the face by the slow months of suppressed anguish and early morning tears. Many an inherited sorrow that has marred a life has been breathed into no human ear.[1]

I want to speak to you tonight about the "inherited sorrows" of women on this Amerikan soil, sorrows which have

Delivered for the National Organization for Women, Washington, D.C., on August 23, 1975, to commemorate the fifty-fifth anniversary of women's suffrage; The Community Church of Boston, November 9, 1975.

marred millions upon millions of human lives, sorrows which have "been breathed into no human ear," or sorrows which were breathed and then forgotten.

This nation's history is one of spilled blood. Everything that has grown here has grown in fields irrigated by the blood of whole peoples. This is a nation built on the human carrion of the Indian nations. This is a nation built on slave labor, slaughter, and grief. This is a racist nation, a sexist nation, a murderous nation. This is a nation pathologically seized by the will to domination.

Fifty-five years ago, we women became citizens of this nation. After seventy years of fierce struggle for suffrage, our kindly lords saw fit to *give* us the vote. Since that time, we have been, at least in a ceremonial way, participants in the blood-letting of our government; we have been implicated formally and officially in its crimes. The hope of our foremothers was this: that when women had the vote, we would use it to stop the crimes of men against men and of men against women. Our foremothers believed that they had given us the tool which would enable us to transform a corrupt nation into a nation of righteousness. It is a bitter thing to say that they were deluded. It is a bitter thing to say that the vote became the tombstone over their obscure graves.

We women do not have many victories to celebrate. Everywhere, our people are in chains—designated as biologically inferior to men; our very bodies controlled by men and male law; the victims of violent, savage crimes; bound by law, custom, and habit to sexual and domestic servitude; exploited mercilessly in any paid labor; robbed of identity and ambition as a condition of birth. We want to claim the vote as a victory. We want to celebrate. We want to rejoice. But the fact is that the vote was only a cosmetic change in our condition. Suffrage has been for us the illusion of participation without the reality of self-determination. We are still a colonialized people, subject to the will of men. And, in fact, behind the vote there is the story of a movement that betrayed itself by abandoning its own visionary insights and compromising its deepest principles. August 26, 1920, signifies, most bitterly, the death of the first feminist movement in Amerika.

How do we celebrate that death? How do we rejoice in the demise of a movement that set out to salvage our lives from the wreck and ruin of patriarchal domination? What victory is there in the dead ash of a feminist movement burned out?

The meaning of the vote is this: that we had better flesh out our invisible past, so that we can understand how and why so much ended in so little; that we had better resurrect our dead, to study how they lived and why they died; that we had better find a cure for whatever disease wiped them out, so that it will not decimate us.

Many women, I think, resist feminism because it is an agony to be fully conscious of the brutal misogyny which permeates culture, society, and all personal relationships. It is as if our oppression were cast in lava eons ago and now it is granite, and each individual woman is buried inside the stone. Women try to survive inside the stone, buried in it. Women say, I like this stone, its weight is not too heavy for me. Women defend the stone by saying that it protects them from rain and wind and fire. Women say, all I have ever known is this stone, what is there without it?

For some women, being buried in the stone is unbearable. They want to move freely. They exert all their strength to claw away at the hard rock that encases them. They rip their fingernails, bruise their fists, tear the skin on their hands until it is raw and bleeding. They rip their lips open on the rock, and break their teeth, and choke on the granite as it crumbles into their mouths. Many women die in this desperate, solitary battle against the stone.

But what if the impulse to freedom were to be born in all of the women buried in the stone? What if the material of the rock itself had become so saturated with the stinking smell of women's rotting bodies, the accumulated stench of thousands of years of decay and death, that no woman could contain her repulsion? What would those women do if, finally, they did want to be free?

I think that they would study the stone. I think that they would use every mental and physical faculty available to them to analyze the stone, its structure, its qualities, its nature, its chemical composition, its density, the physical laws which determine its properties. They would try to discover where it was eroded, what substances could decompose it, what kind of pressure was required to shatter it.

This investigation would require absolute rigor and honesty. Any lie that they told themselves about the nature of the stone would impede their liberation. Any lie that they told themselves about their own condition inside the stone would perpetuate the very situation that had become intolerable to them.

I think that we do not want to be buried inside the stone anymore. I think that the stench of decaying female carcasses has at last become so vile to us that we are ready to face the truth—about the stone, and about ourselves inside it.

(2)

The slavery of women originates thousands of years ago, in a prehistory of civilization which remains inaccessible to us. How women came to be slaves, owned by men, we do not know. We do know that the slavery of women to men is the oldest known form of slavery in the history of the world.

The first slaves brought to this country by Anglo-Saxon imperialists were women—white women. Their slavery was sanctified by religious and civil law, reified by custom and tradition, and enforced by the systematic sadism of men as a slave-owning class.

The rights of women under English law during the seventeenth and eighteenth centuries are described in the following paragraph:

> In this consolidation which we call wedlock is a locking together. It is true, that man and wife are one person; but understand in what manner. When a small brooke or little river incorporateth with . . . the Thames, the poor rivulet looseth her name; it is carried and recarried with the new associate; it beareth no sway; it possesseth nothing . . . A woman as soon as she is married, is called *covert* [covered]; in Latine *nupta*, that is, "veiled"; as it were, clouded and overshadowed; she hath lost her streame. . . . Her new self is her superior; her companion, her master . . . Eve, because she helped to seduce her husband, had inflicted upon her a special bane. See here the reason . . . that women have no voice in Parliament. They make no laws, they consent to none, they abrogate none. All of them are understood either married, or to be married, and their desires are to their husbands. . . . The common laws here shaketh hand with divinitye.[2]

English law obtained in the colonies. There was no new world here for women.

Women were sold into marriage in the colonies, first for the price of passage from England; then, as men began to accrue wealth, for larger sums, paid to merchants who sold women as if they were potatoes.

Women were imported into the colonies to breed. Just as a man bought land so that he could grow food, he bought a wife so that he could grow sons.

A man owned his wife and all that she produced. Her crop came from her womb, and this crop was harvested year after year until she died.

According to law, a man even owned a woman's unborn children. He also owned any personal property she might have —her clothing, hairbrushes, all personal effects however insignificant. He also, of course, had the right to her labor as a domestic, and owned all that she made with her hands—food, clothing, textiles, etc.

A man had the right of corporal punishment, or "chastisement" as it was then called. Wives were whipped and beaten for disobedience, or on whim, with the full sanction of law and custom.

A wife who ran away was a fugitive slave. She could be hunted down, returned to her owner, and brutally punished by being jailed or whipped. Anyone who aided her in her escape, or who gave her food or shelter, could be prosecuted for robbery.

Marriage was a tomb. Once inside it, a woman was civilly dead. She had no political rights, no private rights, no personal rights. She was owned, body and soul, by her husband. Even when he died, she could not inherit the children she had birthed; a husband was required to bequeath his children to another male who would then have the full rights of custody and guardianship.

Most white women, of course, were brought to the colonies as married chattel. A smaller group of white women, however, were brought over as indentured servants. Theoretically, indentured servants were contracted into servitude for a specified amount of time, usually in exchange for the price of passage. But, in fact, the time of servitude could be easily extended by the master as a punishment for infraction of rules or laws. For example, it often happened that an indentured servant, who had no legal or economic means of protection by definition, would be used sexually by her master, impregnated, then accused of having borne a bastard, which was a crime. The punishment for this crime would be an additional sentence of service to her master. One argument used to justify this abuse was that pregnancy had lessened the woman's usefulness, so that the master had been cheated of labor. The woman was compelled to make good on his loss.

Female slavery in England, then in Amerika, was not structurally different from female slavery anywhere else in the world. The institutional oppression of women is not the product of a discrete historical time, nor is it derived from a particular national circumstance, nor is it limited to Western culture, nor is it the consequence of a particular economic system. Female slavery in Amerika was congruent with the universal character of abject female subjugation: women were carnal chattel; their bodies and all their biological issue were owned by men; the domination of men over them was systematic, sadistic, and sexual in its origins; their slavery was the base on which all social life was built and the model from which all other forms of social domination were derived.

The atrocity of male domination over women poisoned the social body, in Amerika as elsewhere. The first to die from this poison, of course, were women—their genius destroyed; every human potential diminished; their strength ravaged; their bodies plundered; their will trampled by their male masters.

But the will to domination is a ravenous beast. There are never enough warm bodies to satiate its monstrous hunger. Once alive, this beast grows and grows, feeding on all the life around it, scouring the earth to find new sources of nourishment. This beast lives in each man who battens on female servitude.

Every married man, no matter how poor, owned one slave —his wife. Every married man, no matter how powerless compared to other men, had absolute power over one slave— his wife. Every married man, no matter what his rank in the world of men, was tyrant and master over one woman—his wife.

And every man, married or not, had a gender class consciousness of his right to domination over women, to brutal and absolute authority over the bodies of women, to ruthless and malicious tyranny over the hearts, minds, and destinies of women. This right to sexual domination was a birthright, predicated on the will of God, fixed by the known laws of biology, not subject to modification or to the restraint of law or reason. Every man, married or not, knew that he was not a woman, not carnal chattel, not an animal put on earth to be fucked and to breed. This knowledge was the center of his identity, the source of his pride, the germ of his power.

It was, then, no contradiction or moral agony to begin to buy black slaves. The will to domination had battened on female flesh; its muscles had grown strong and firm in subjugating women; its lust for power had become frenzied in the sadistic pleasure of absolute supremacy. Whatever dimension of human conscience must atrophy before men can turn other humans into chattel had become shriveled and useless long before the first black slaves were imported into the English colonies. Once female slavery is established as the diseased groundwork of a society, racist and other hierarchical pathologies inevitably develop from it.

There was a slave trade in blacks which pre-dated the English colonialization of what is now the eastern United States. During the Middle Ages, there were black slaves in Europe in comparatively small numbers. It was the Portuguese who first really devoted themselves to the abduction and sale of blacks. They developed the Atlantic slave trade. Black slaves were imported in massive quantities into Portuguese, Spanish, French, Dutch, Danish, and Swedish colonies.

In the English colonies, as I have said, every married man had one slave, his wife. As men accrued wealth, they bought more slaves, black slaves, who were already being brought across the Atlantic to be sold into servitude. A man's wealth has always been measured by how much he owns. A man buys property both to increase his wealth and to demonstrate his wealth. Black slaves were bought for both these purposes.

The laws which fixed the chattel status of white women were now extended to apply to the black slave. The divine right which had sanctioned the slavery of women to men was now interpreted to make the slavery of blacks to white men a function of God's will. The malicious notion of biological inferiority, which originated to justify the abject subjugation of women to men, was now expanded to justify the abject subjugation of blacks to whites. The whip, used to cut the backs of white women to ribbons, was now wielded against black flesh as well.

Black men and black women were both kidnapped from their African homes and sold into slavery, but their condition in slavery differed in kind. The white man perpetuated his view of female inferiority in the institution of black slavery. The value of the black male slave in the marketplace was double the value of the black female slave; his labor in the field or in the house was calculated to be worth twice hers.

The condition of the black woman in slavery was determined first by her sex, then by her race. The nature of her servitude differed from that of the black male because she was carnal chattel, a sexual commodity, subject to the sexual will of her white master. In the field or in the house, she endured the same conditions as the male slave. She worked as hard; she worked as long; her food and clothing were as inadequate; her superiors wielded the whip against her as often. But the black woman was bred like a beast of burden, whether the stud who mounted her was her white master or a black slave of his choosing. Her economic worth, always less than that of a black male, was measured first by her capacity as a breeder to produce more wealth in the form of more slaves for the master; then by her capacities as a field or house slave.

As black slaves were imported into the English colonies, the character of white female slavery was altered in a very bizarre way. Wives remained chattel. Their purpose was still to produce sons year after year until they died. But their male masters, in an ecstasy of domination, put their bodies to a new use: they were to be ornaments, utterly useless, utterly passive, decorative objects kept to demonstrate the surplus wealth of the master.

This creation of woman-as-ornament can be observed in all societies predicated on female slavery where men have accumulated wealth. In China, for instance, where for a thousand years women's feet were bound, the poor woman's feet were bound loosely—she still had to work; her feet were bound, her husband's were not; that made him superior to her because he could walk faster than she could; but still, she had to produce the children and raise them, do the domestic labor, and often work in the fields as well; he could not afford to cripple her completely because he needed her labor. But the woman who was wife to the rich man was immobilized; her feet were reduced to stumps so that she was utterly useless, except as a fuck and a breeder. The degree of her uselessness signified the degree of his wealth. Absolute physical crippling was the height of female fashion, the ideal of feminine beauty, the erotic touchstone of female identity.

In Amerika as elsewhere, physical bondage was the real purpose of high feminine fashion. The lady's costume was a sadistic invention designed to abuse her body. Her ribs were pushed up and in; her waist was squeezed to its tiniest possible size so that she would resemble an hourglass; her skirts were wide and very heavy. The movements that she could make in this constraining and often painful attire were regarded as the essence of feminine grace. Ladies fainted so often because they could not breathe. Ladies were so passive because they could not move.

Also, of course, ladies were trained to mental and moral idiocy. Any display of intelligence compromised a lady's value as an ornament. Any assertion of principled will contradicted her master's definition of her as a decorative object. Any rebellion against the mindless passivity which the slave-owning class had articulated as her true nature could incur the wrath of her powerful owner and bring on her censure and ruin.

The expensive gowns which adorned the lady, her leisure, and her vacuity have obscured for many the cold, hard reality of her status as carnal chattel. Since her function was to signify male wealth, it is often assumed that she possessed that wealth. In fact, she was a breeder and an ornament, with no private or political rights, with no claim either to dignity or freedom.

The genius of any slave system is found in the dynamics which isolate slaves from each other, obscure the reality of a common condition, and make united rebellion against the oppressor inconceivable. The power of the master is absolute and incontrovertible. His authority is protected by civil law, armed force, custom, and divine and/or biological sanction.

Slaves characteristically internalize the oppressor's view of them, and this internalized view congeals into a pathological self-hatred. Slaves typically learn to hate the qualities and behaviors which characterize their own group and to identify their own self-interest with the self-interest of their oppressor. The master's position at the top is invulnerable; one aspires to become the master, or to become close to the master, or to be recognized by virtue of one's good service to the master. Resentment, rage, and bitterness at one's own powerlessness cannot be directed upward against him, so it is all directed against other slaves who are the living embodiment of one's own degradation.

Among women, this dynamic works itself out in what Phyllis Chesler has called "harem politics."[3] The first wife is tyrant over the second wife who is tyrant over the third wife, etc.

The authority of the first wife, or any other woman in the harem who has prerogatives over other women, is a function of her powerlessness in relation to the master. The labor that she does as a fuck and as a breeder can be done by any other woman of her gender class. She, in common with all other women of her abused class, is instantly replaceable. This means that whatever acts of cruelty she commits against other women are done as the agent of the master. Her behavior inside the harem over and against other women is in the interest of her master, whose dominance is fixed by the hatred of women for each other.

Inside the harem, removed from all access to real power, robbed of any possibility of self-determination, all women typically act out on other women their repressed rage against the master; and they also act out their internalized hatred of their own kind. Again, this effectively secures the master's dominance, since women divided against each other will not unite against him.

In the domain of the owner of black slaves, the white woman was the first wife, but the master had many other concubines, actually or potentially—black women slaves. The white wife became her husband's agent against these other carnal chattel. Her rage against her owner could only be taken out on them, which it was, often ruthlessly and brutally. Her hatred of her own kind was acted out on those who, like her, were carnal chattel, but who, unlike her, were black. She also, of course, aggressed against her own white daughters by binding and shackling them as ladies, forcing them to develop the passivity of ornaments, and endorsing the institution of marriage.

Black women slaves, on whose bodies the carnage of white male dominance was visited most savagely, had lives of unrelieved bitterness. They did backbreaking labor; their children were taken from them and sold; they were the sexual servants of their masters; and they often bore the wrath of white women humiliated into cruelty by the conditions of their own servitude.

Harem politics, the self-hatred of the oppressed which wreaks vengeance on its own kind, and the tendency of the slave to identify her own self-interest with the self-interest of the master—all conspired to make it impossible for white women, black women, and black men to understand the astonishing similarities in their conditions and to unite against their common oppressor.

Now, there are many who believe that changes occur in society because of disembodied processes: they describe change in terms of technological advances; or they paint giant pictures of abstract forces clashing in thin air. But I think that we as women know that there are no disembodied processes; that all history originates in human flesh; that all oppression is inflicted by the body of one against the body of another; that all social change is built on the bone and muscle, and out of the flesh and blood, of human creators.

Two such creators were the Grimké sisters of Charleston, South Carolina. Sarah, born in 1792, was the sixth of fourteen children; Angelina, born in 1805, was the last. Their father was a rich lawyer who owned numerous black slaves.

Early in her childhood, Sarah rebelled against her own condition as a lady and against the ever-present horror of black slavery. Her earliest ambition was to become a lawyer, but education was denied her by her outraged father who wanted her only to dance, flirt, and marry. "With me learning was a passion," she wrote later. "My nature [was] denied her appropriate nutriment, her course counteracted, her aspirations crushed."[4] In her adolescence, Sarah conscientiously defied the Southern law that prohibited teaching slaves to read. She gave reading lessons in the slave Sunday school until she was discovered by her father; and even after that, she continued to tutor her own maid. "The light was put out," she wrote, "the keyhole screened, and flat on our stomachs, before the fire, with the spelling-book under our eyes, we defied the laws of South Carolina."[5] Eventually, this too was discovered, and understanding that the maid would be whipped for further infractions, Sarah ended the reading lessons.

In 1821, Sarah left the South and went to Philadelphia. She renounced her family's Episcopal religion and became a Quaker.

Angelina, too, could not tolerate black slavery. In 1829, at the age of twenty-four, she wrote in her diary: "That system must be radically wrong which can only be supported by transgressing the laws of God."[6] In 1828, she too moved to Philadelphia.

In 1835, Angelina wrote a personal letter to William Lloyd Garrison, the militant abolitionist. She wrote: "The ground upon which you stand is holy ground: never—never surrender it. If you surrender it, the hope of the slave is extinguished. . . . [I]t is my deep, solemn deliberate conviction, that this is a cause worth dying for."[7] Garrison published the letter in his abolitionist paper, *The Liberator*, with a foreword identifying Angelina as the member of a prominent slaveholding family. She was widely condemned by friends and acquaintances for disgracing her family, and Sarah, too, condemned her.

In 1836, she sealed her fate as a traitor to her race and to her family by publishing an abolitionist tract called "An Appeal to the Christian Women of the South." For the first time, maybe in the history of the world, a woman addressed other women and demanded that they unite as a revolutionary force to overthrow a system of tyranny. And for the first time on Amerikan soil, a woman demanded that white women identify themselves with the welfare, freedom, and dignity of black women:

> Let [women] embody themselves in societies, and send petitions up to their different legislatures, entreating their husbands, fathers, brothers, and sons, to abolish the institution of slavery; no longer to subject *woman* to the scourge and the chain, to mental darkness and moral degradation; no longer to tear husbands from their wives, and children from their parents; no longer to make men, women, and children, work *without wages*; no longer to make their lives bitter in hard bondage; no longer to reduce *American citizens* to the abject condition of *slaves*, of "chattels personal;" no longer to barter the *image of God* in human shambles for corruptible things such as silver and gold.[8]

Angelina exhorted white Southern women, for the sake of all women, to form antislavery societies; to petition legislatures; to educate themselves to the harsh realities of black slavery; to speak out against black slavery to family, friends, and acquaintances; to demand that slaves be freed in their own families; to pay wages to any slaves who are not freed; to act against the law by freeing slaves wherever possible; and to act against the law by teaching slaves to read and to write. In the first political articulation of civil disobedience as a principle of action, she wrote:

> But some of you will say, we can neither free our slaves nor teach them to read, for the laws of our state forbid it. Be not surprised when I say such wicked laws *ought to be no barrier* in the way of your duty . . . If a law commands me to *sin I will break it*; if it calls me to *suffer*, I will let it take its course *unresistingly*. The doctrine of blind obedience and unqualified sub-

mission to *any human power*, whether civil or ecclesiastical, is the doctrine of despotism . . .[9]

This tract was burned by Southern postmasters; Angelina was warned in newspaper editorials never to return to the South; and she was repudiated by her family. After the publication of her "Appeal," she became a full-time abolitionist organizer.

Also in 1836, in a series of letters to Catherine Beecher, Angelina articulated the first fully conceived feminist argument against the oppression of women:

Now, I believe it is woman's right to have a choice in all the laws and regulations by which she is to be *governed*, whether in Church or State; and that the present arrangements of society . . . are a *violation of human rights, a rank usurpation of power*, a violent seizure and confiscation of what is sacredly and inalienably hers—thus inflicting upon woman outrageous wrongs, working mischief incalculable in the social circle, and in its influence on the world producing only evil, and that continually.[10]

Her feminist consciousness had grown out of her abolitionist commitment: "The investigation of the rights of the slave has led me to a better understanding of my own."[11]

Also in 1836, Sarah Grimké published a pamphlet called "Epistle to the Clergy of the Southern States." In it, she refutes the claims by Southern clergy that biblical slavery provided a justification for Amerikan slavery. From this time on, Sarah and Angelina were united publicly and privately in their political work.

In 1837, the Grimké sisters attended an antislavery convention in New York City. There they asserted that white and black women were a sisterhood; that the institution of black slavery was nourished by Northern race prejudice; and that white women and black men also shared a common condition:

[The female slaves] are our countrywomen—*they are our sisters*; and to us as women, they have a right to look for sympathy with their sorrows, and effort and prayer for their rescue . . . Our people have erected a false standard by which to judge man's character. Because in the slave-holding States colored men are plundered and kept in abject ignorance, are treated with disdain and scorn, so here, too in profound deference to the South, we refuse to eat, or ride, or walk, or associate, or open our institutions of learning, or even our zoological institutions to people of color, unless they visit them in the capacity of *servants*, of menials in humble attendance upon the Anglo-American. Who ever heard of a more wicked absurdity in a Republican country?

Women ought to feel a peculiar sympathy in the colored man's wrongs, for, like him, she has been accused of mental inferiority, and denied the privileges of a liberal education.[12]

In 1837, public reaction against the Grimké sisters became fierce. The Massachusetts clergy published a pastoral letter denouncing female activism:

We invite your attention to the dangers which at present seem to threaten the female character with wide-spread and permanent injury.

... We cannot ... but regret the mistaken conduct of those who encourage females to bear an obtrusive and ostentatious part in measures of reform, and [we cannot] countenance any of that sex who so far forget themselves as to itinerate in the character of public lecturers and teachers. We especially deplore the intimate acquaintance and promiscuous conversation of females with regard to things which ought not to be named; by which that modesty and delicacy which is the charm of domestic life, and which constitutes the true influence of woman in society, is consumed, and the way opened, as we apprehend, for degeneracy and ruin.[13]

Replying to the pastoral letter, Angelina wrote: "We are placed very unexpectedly in a very trying situation, in the forefront of an entirely new contest—a contest for the *rights of woman* as a moral, intelligent and responsible being."[14] Sarah's reply, which was later published as part of a systematic analysis of women's oppression called *Letters on the Equality of the Sexes and the Condition of Women*, read in part as follows:

[The pastoral letter] says, "We invite your attention to the dangers which at present seem to threaten the FEMALE CHARACTER with wide-spread and permanent injury." I rejoice that they have called the attention of my sex to this subject, because I believe if woman investigates it, she will soon discover that danger is impending, though from a totally different source . . . danger from those who, having long held the reins of *usurped* authority, are unwilling to permit us to fill that sphere which God created us to move in, and who have entered into league to crush the immortal mind of woman. I rejoice, because I am persuaded that the rights of woman, like the rights of slaves, need only be examined to be understood and asserted, even by some of those who are now endeavoring to smother the irrepressible desire for mental and spiritual freedom which glows in the breast of many, who hardly dare to speak their sentiments.[15]

In this confrontation with the Massachusetts clergy, the women's rights movement was born in the United States. Two women, speaking for all the oppressed of their kind, resolved to transform society in the name of, and for the sake of, women. The work of Angelina and Sarah Grimké, so profound in its political analysis of tyranny, so visionary in its revolutionary urgency, so unyielding in its hatred of human bondage, so radical in its perception of the common oppression of all women and black men, was the fiber from which the cloth of the first feminist movement was woven. Elizabeth Cady Stanton, Lucretia Mott, Susan B. Anthony, Lucy Stone —these were the daughters of the Grimké sisters, birthed through their miraculous labor.

It is often said that all those who advocated women's rights were abolitionists, but that not all abolitionists advocated women's rights. The bitter truth is that most male abolitionists opposed women's rights. Frederick Douglass, a former black slave who strongly supported women's rights, described this opposition in 1848, right after the Seneca Falls Convention:

A discussion of the rights of animals would be regarded with far more complacency by many of what are called the *wise* and the *good* of our land, than would be a discussion of the rights of women. It is, in their estimation, to be guilty of evil thoughts, to think that woman is entitled to equal rights with man. Many who have at last made the discovery that the negroes have some rights as well as other members of the human family, have yet to be convinced that women are entitled to any. . . . [A] number of persons of this description actually abandoned the anti-slavery cause, lest by giving their influence in that direction they might possibly be giving countenance to the dangerous heresy that woman, in respect to her rights, stands on an equal footing with man. In the judgment of such persons, the American slave system, with all its concomitant horrors, is less to be deplored than this *wicked* idea.[16]

In the abolition movement as in most movements for social change, then and now, women were the committed; women did the work that had to be done; women were the backbone and muscle that supported the whole body. But when women made claims for their own rights, they were dismissed contemptuously, ridiculed, or told that their own struggle was self-indulgent, secondary to the real struggle. As Elizabeth Cady Stanton wrote in her reminiscences:

During the six years [of the Civil War, when women] held their own claims in abeyance to those of the slaves . . . and labored to inspire the people with enthusiasm for [emancipation] they were highly honored as "wise, loyal, and clearsighted." But when the slaves were emancipated, and these women asked that they should be recognized in the reconstruction as citizens of the Republic, equal before the law, all these transcendent virtues vanished like dew before the morning sun. And thus it ever is: so long as woman labors to second man's endeavors and exalt his sex above her own her virtues pass unquestioned; but when she dares to demand rights and privileges for herself, her motives, manners, dress, personal appearance, and character are subjects for ridicule and detraction.[17]

Women had, as Stanton pointed out, "stood with the negro, thus far, on equal ground as ostracized classes, outside the political paradise";[18] but most male abolitionists, and the

Republican party which came to represent them, had no commitment to the civil rights of women, let alone to the radical social transformation demanded by feminists. These male abolitionists had, instead, a commitment to male dominance, an investment in male privilege, and a sustaining belief in male supremacy.

In 1868, the Fourteenth Amendment which enfranchised black men was ratified. In this very amendment, the word "male" was introduced into the United States Constitution for the first time—this to insure that the Fourteenth Amendment would not, even accidentally, license suffrage or other legal rights for women.

This betrayal was contemptible. Abolitionist men had betrayed the very women whose organizing, lecturing, and pamphleteering had effected abolition. Abolitionist men had betrayed one half the population of former black slaves—black women who had no civil existence under the Fourteenth Amendment. Black men joined with white men to deny black women civil rights. Abolitionists joined with former slaveholders; former male slaves joined with former slaveholders; white and black men joined together to close male ranks against white and black women. The consequences for the black woman were as Sojourner Truth prophesied in 1867, one year after the Fourteenth Amendment was proposed:

> I come from . . . the country of the slave. They have got their liberty—so much good luck to have slavery partly destroyed; not entirely. I want it root and branch destroyed. Then we will all be free indeed. . . . There is a great stir about colored men getting their rights, but not a word about the colored women; and if colored men get their rights, and not colored women theirs, you see the colored men will be masters over the women, and it will be just as bad as it was before.[19]

If slavery is ever to be destroyed "root and branch," women will have to destroy it. Men, as their history attests, will only pluck its buds and pick its flowers.

I want to ask you to commit yourselves to your own freedom; I want to ask you not to settle for anything less, not to compromise, not to barter, not to be deceived by empty promises and cruel lies. I want to remind you that slavery must be destroyed "root and branch," or it has not been destroyed at all. I want to ask you to remember that we have been slaves for so long that sometimes we forget that we are not free. I want to remind you that we are not free. I want to ask you to commit yourselves to a women's revolution—a revolution of all women, by all women, and for all women; a revolution aimed at digging out the roots of tyranny so that it cannot grow anymore.

9

The Root Cause

> And the things best to know are first principles and causes. For through them and from them all other things may be known...
> —Aristotle, *Metaphysics,* Book I

I want to talk to you tonight about some realities and some possibilities. The realities are brutal and savage; the possibilities may seem to you, quite frankly, impossible. I want to remind you that there was a time when everyone believed that the earth was flat. All navigation was based on this belief. All maps were drawn to the specifications of this belief. I call it a belief, but then it was a reality, the only imaginable reality. It was a reality because everyone believed it to be true. Everyone believed it to be true because it appeared to be true. The earth *looked* flat; there was no circumstance in which it did not have, in the distances, edges off which one might fall; people assumed that, somewhere, there was the final edge beyond which there was nothing. Imagination was circumscribed, as it most often is, by inherently limited and culturally conditioned physical senses, and those senses determined that the earth was flat. This principle of reality was not only theoretical; it was acted on. Ships never sailed too far in any direction because no one wanted to sail off the edge of the earth; no one wanted to die the dreadful death that would result from such a

Delivered at the Massachusetts Institute of Technology, Cambridge, September, 26, 1975.

reckless, stupid act. In societies in which navigation was a major activity, the fear of such a fate was vivid and terrifying.

Now, as the story goes, somehow a man named Christopher Columbus imagined that the earth was round. He imagined that one could reach the Far East by sailing west. How he conceived of this idea, we do not know; but he did imagine it, and once he had imagined it, he could not forget it. For a long time, until he met Queen Isabella, no one would listen to him or consider his idea because, clearly, he was a lunatic. If anything was certain, it was that the earth was flat. Now we look at pictures of the earth taken from outer space, and we do not remember that once there was a universal belief that the earth was flat.

This story has been repeated many times. Marie Curie got the peculiar idea that there was an undiscovered element which was active, ever-changing, alive. All scientific thought was based on the notion that all the elements were inactive, inert, stable. Ridiculed, denied a proper laboratory by the scientific establishment, condemned to poverty and obscurity, Marie Curie, with her husband, Pierre, worked relentlessly to isolate radium which was, in the first instance, a figment of her imagination. The discovery of radium entirely destroyed the basic premise on which both physics and chemistry were built. What had been real until its discovery was real no longer.

The known tried-and-true principles of reality, then, universally believed and adhered to with a vengeance, are often shaped out of profound ignorance. We do not know what or how much we do not know. Ignoring our ignorance, even though it has been revealed to us time and time again, we believe that reality is whatever we do know.

One basic principle of reality, universally believed and adhered to with a vengeance, is that there are two sexes, man and woman, and that these sexes are not only distinct from each other, but are opposite. The model often used to describe the nature of these two sexes is that of magnetic poles. The male sex is likened to the positive pole, and the female sex is likened to the negative pole. Brought into proximity with each other, the magnetic fields of these two sexes are supposed to interact, locking the two poles together into a perfect whole. Needless to say, two like poles brought into proximity are supposed to repel each other.

The male sex, in keeping with its positive designation, has positive qualities; and the female sex, in keeping with its negative designation, does not have any of the positive qualities attributed to the male sex. For instance, according to this model, men are active, strong, and courageous; and women are passive, weak, and fearful. In other words, whatever men are, women are not; whatever men can do, women cannot do; whatever capacities men have, women do not have. Man is the positive and woman is his negative.

Apologists for this model claim that it is moral because it is inherently egalitarian. Each pole is supposed to have the dignity of its own separate identity; each pole is necessary to a harmonious whole. This notion, of course, is rooted in the conviction that the claims made as to the character of each sex are *true,* that the essence of each sex is accurately described. In other words, to say that man is the positive and woman is the negative is like saying that sand is dry and water is wet— the characteristic which most describes the thing itself is named in a true way and no judgment on the worth of these differing characteristics is implied. Simone de Beauvoir exposes the fallacy of this "separate but equal" doctrine in the preface to *The Second Sex*:

> In actuality the relation of the two sexes is not . . . like that of two electrical poles, for man represents both the positive and the neutral, as is indicated by the common use of *man* to designate human beings in general; whereas woman represents only the negative, defined by limiting criteria, without reciprocity. . . . "The female is a female by virtue of a certain *lack* of qualities," said Aristotle; "we should regard the female nature as afflicted with a natural defectiveness." And St. Thomas for his part pro-

nounced woman to be "an imperfect man," an "incidental" being...

Thus, humanity is male and man defines woman not in herself but as relative to him; she is not regarded as an autonomous being.[1]

This diseased view of woman as the negative of man, "female by virtue of a certain *lack* of qualities," infects the whole of culture. It is the cancer in the gut of every political and economic system, of every social institution. It is the rot which spoils all human relationships, infests all human psychological reality, and destroys the very fiber of human identity.

This pathological view of female negativity has been enforced on our flesh for thousands of years. The savage mutilation of the female body, undertaken to distinguish us absolutely from men, has occurred on a massive scale. For instance, in China, for one thousand years, women's feet were reduced to stumps through footbinding. When a girl was seven or eight years old, her feet were washed in alum, a chemical that causes shrinkage. Then, all toes but the big toes were bent into the soles of her feet and bandaged as tightly as possible. This procedure was repeated over and over again for approximately three years. The girl, in agony, was forced to walk on her feet. Hard calluses formed; toenails grew into the skin; the feet were pus-filled and bloody; circulation was virtually stopped; often the big toes fell off. The ideal foot was three inches of smelly, rotting flesh. Men were positive and women were negative because men could walk and women could not. Men were strong and women were weak because men could walk and women could not. Men were independent and women were dependent because men could walk and women could not. Men were virile because women were crippled.

This atrocity committed against Chinese women is only one example of the systematic sadism acted out on the bodies of women to render us opposite to, and the negatives of, men. We have been, and are, whipped, beaten, and assaulted; we have been, and are, encased in clothing designed to distort our bodies, to make movement and breathing painful and difficult; we have been, and are, turned into ornaments, so deprived of physical presence that we cannot run or jump or climb or even walk with a natural posture; we have been, and are, veiled, our faces covered by layers of suffocating cloth or by layers of make-up, so that even possession of our own faces is denied us; we have been, and are, forced to remove the hair from our armpits, legs, eyebrows, and often even from our pubic areas, so that men can assert, without contradiction, the positivity of their own hairy virility. We have been, and are, sterilized against our will; our wombs are removed for no medical reason; our clitorises are cut off; our breasts and the whole musculature of our chests are removed with enthusiastic abandon. This last procedure, radical mastectomy, is eighty years old. I ask you to consider the development of weaponry in the last eighty years, nuclear bombs, poisonous gases, laser beams, noise bombs, and the like, and to question the development of technology in relation to women. Why are women still being mutilated so promiscuously in breast surgery; why has this savage form of mutilation, radical mastectomy, thrived if not to enhance the negativity of women in relation to men? These forms of physical mutilation are *brands* which designate us as female by negating our very bodies, by destroying them.

In the bizarre world made by men, the primary physical emblem of female negativity is pregnancy. Women have the capacity to bear children; men do not. But since men are positive and women are negative, the inability to bear children is designated as a positive characteristic, and the ability to bear children is designated as a negative characteristic. Since women are most easily distinguished from men by virtue of this single capacity, and since the negativity of women is always established in opposition to the positivity of men, the childbearing capacity of the female is used first to fix, then to confirm, her negative or inferior status. Pregnancy becomes a physical brand, a sign designating the pregnant one as authentically female. Childbearing, peculiarly, becomes the form and substance of female negativity.

Again, consider technology in relation to women. As men walk on the moon and a man-made satellite approaches Mars for a landing, the technology of contraception remains criminally inadequate. The two most effective means of contraception are the pill and the I.U.D. The pill is poisonous and the I.U.D. is sadistic. Should a woman want to prevent conception, she must either fail eventually because she uses an ineffective method of contraception, in which case she risks death through childbearing; or she must risk dreadful disease with the pill, or suffer agonizing pain with the I.U.D.—and, of course, with either of these methods, the risk of death is also very real. Now that abortion techniques have been developed which are safe and easy, women are resolutely denied free access to them. Men require that women continue to become pregnant so as to embody female negativity, thus confirming male positivity.

While the physical assaults against female life are staggering, the outrages committed against our intellectual and creative faculties have been no less sadistic. Consigned to a negative intellectual and creative life, so as to affirm these capacities in men, women are considered to be mindless; femininity is roughly synonymous with stupidity. We are feminine to the degree that our mental faculties are annihilated or repudiated. To enforce this dimension of female negativity, we are systematically denied access to formal education, and every assertion of natural intelligence is punished until we do not dare to trust our perceptions, until we do not dare to honor our creative impulses, until we do not dare to exercise our critical faculties, until we do not dare to cultivate our imaginations, until we do not dare to respect our own mental or moral acuity. Whatever creative or intellectual work we do manage to do is trivialized, ignored, or ridiculed, so that even those few whose minds could not be degraded are driven to suicide or insanity, or back into marriage and childbearing. There are very few exceptions to this inexorable rule.

The most vivid literary manifestation of this pathology of female negation is found in pornography. Literature is always the most eloquent expression of cultural values; and pornography articulates the purest distillation of those values. In literary pornography, where female blood can flow without the real restraint of biological endurance, the ethos of this murderous male-positive culture is revealed in its skeletal form: male sadism feeds on female masochism; male dominance is nourished by female submission.

In pornography, sadism is the means by which men establish their dominance. Sadism is the authentic exercise of power which confirms manhood; and the first characteristic of manhood is that its existence is based on the negation of the female —manhood can only be certified by abject female degradation, a degradation never abject enough until the victim's body and will have both been destroyed.

In literary pornography, the pulsating heart of darkness at the center of the male-positive system is exposed in all of its terrifying nakedness. That heart of darkness is this—that sexual sadism actualizes male identity. Women are tortured, whipped, and chained; women are bound and gagged, branded and burned, cut with knives and wires; women are pissed on and shit on; red-hot needles are driven into breasts, bones are broken, rectums are torn, mouths are ravaged, cunts are savagely bludgeoned by penis after penis, dildo after dildo—and all of this to establish in the male a viable sense of his own worth.

Typically in pornography, some of this gruesome cruelty takes place in a public context. A man has not thoroughly mastered a woman—he is not thoroughly a man—until her degradation is publicly witnessed and enjoyed. In other words, as a man establishes dominance he must also publicly establish ownership. Ownership is proven when a man can humiliate a woman in front of, and for the pleasure of, his fellows, and still she remains loyal to him. Ownership is further established when a man can loan a woman out as a carnal object, or give her as a gift to another man or to other men. These transactions make his ownership a matter of public record and in-

The Root Cause

crease his esteem in the eyes of other men. These transactions prove that he has not only claimed absolute authority over her body, but that he has also entirely mastered her will. What might have begun for the woman as submission to a particular man out of "love" for him—and what was in that sense congruent with her own integrity as she could recognize it—must end in the annihilation of even that claim to individuality. The individuality of ownership—"I am the one who owns"—is claimed by the man; but nothing must be left to the woman or in the woman on which she could base any claim to personal dignity, even the shabby dignity of believing, "I am the exclusive property of the man who degrades me." In the same way, and for the same reasons, she is forced to watch the man who possesses her exercising his sexual sadism against other women. This robs her of that internal grain of dignity that comes from believing, "I am the only one," or "I am perceived and my singular identity is verified when he degrades *me*," or "I am distinguished from other women because this man has chosen me."

The pornography of male sadism almost always contains an idealized, or unreal, view of male fellowship. The utopian male concept which is the premise of male pornography is this—since manhood is established and confirmed over and against the brutalized bodies of women, men need not aggress against each other; in other words, women absorb male aggression so that men are safe from it. Each man, knowing his own deep-rooted impulse to savagery, presupposes this same impulse in other men and seeks to protect himself from it. The rituals of male sadism over and against the bodies of women are the means by which male aggression is *socialized* so that a man can associate with other men without the imminent danger of male aggression against his own person. The common erotic project of destroying women makes it possible for men to unite into a brotherhood; this project is the only firm and trustworthy groundwork for cooperation among males and all male bonding is based on it.

is idealized view of male fellowship exposes the essentially homosexual character of male society. Men use women's bodies to form alliances or bonds with each other. Men use women's bodies to achieve recognizable power which will certify male identity in the eyes of other men. Men use women's bodies to enable them to engage in civil and peaceable social transactions with each other. We think that we live in a heterosexual society because most men are fixated on women as sexual objects; but, in fact, we live in a homosexual society because all credible transactions of power, authority, and authenticity take place among men; all transactions based on equity and individuality take place among men. Men are real; therefore, all real relationship is between men; all real communication is between men; all real reciprocity is between men; all real mutuality is between men. Heterosexuality, which can be defined as the sexual dominance of men over women, is like an acorn—from it grows the mighty oak of the male homosexual society, a society of men, by men, and for men, a society in which the positivity of male community is realized through the negation of the female, through the annihilation of women's flesh and will.

In literary pornography, which is a distillation of life as we know it, women are gaping holes, hot slits, fuck tubes, and the like. The female body is supposed to consist of three empty holes, all of which were expressly designed to be filled with erect male positivity.

The female life-force itself is characterized as a negative one: we are defined as inherently masochistic; that is, we are driven toward pain and abuse, toward self-destruction, toward annihilation—and this drive toward our own negation is precisely what identifies us as women. In other words, we are born so that we may be destroyed. Sexual masochism actualizes female negativity, just as sexual sadism actualizes male positivity. A woman's erotic femininity is measured by the degree to which she needs to be hurt, needs to be possessed, needs to be abused, needs to submit, needs to be beaten, needs

The Root Cause

to be humiliated, needs to be degraded. Any woman who resists acting out these so-called needs, or any woman who rebels against the values inherent in these needs, or any woman who refuses to sanction or participate in her own destruction is characterized as a deviant, one who denies her femininity, a shrew, a bitch, etc. Typically, such deviants are brought back into the female flock by rape, gang rape, or some form of bondage. The theory is that once such women have tasted the intoxicating sweetness of submission they will, like lemmings, rush to their own destruction.

Romantic love, in pornography as in life, is the mythic celebration of female negation. For a woman, love is defined as her willingness to submit to her own annihilation. As the saying goes, women are made for love—that is, submission. Love, or submission, must be both the substance and purpose of a woman's life. For the female, the capacity to love is exactly synonymous with the capacity to sustain abuse and the appetite for it. For the woman, the proof of love is that she is willing to be destroyed by the one whom she loves, for his sake. For the woman, love is always self-sacrifice, the sacrifice of identity, will, and bodily integrity, in order to fulfill and redeem the masculinity of her lover.

In pornography, we see female love raw, its naked erotic skeleton; we can almost touch the bones of our dead. Love *is* the erotic masochistic drive; *love is* the frenzied passion which compels a woman to submit to a diminishing life in chains; love *is* the consuming sexual impulse toward degradation and abuse. The woman does literally *give* herself to the man; he does literally *take* and *possess* her.

The primary transaction which expresses this female submission and this male possession, in pornography as in life, is the act of fucking. Fucking is the basic physical expression of male positivity and female negativity. The relationship of sadist to masochist does not originate in the act of fucking; rather, it is expressed and renewed there.

For the male, fucking is a compulsive act, in pornography

and in real life. But in real life, and not in pornography, it is an act fraught with danger, filled with dread. That sanctified organ of male positivity, the phallus, penetrates into the female void. During penetration, the male's whole being *is* his penis—it and his will to domination are entirely one; the erect penis is his identity; all sensation is localized in the penis and in effect the rest of his body is insensate, dead. During penetration, a male's very being is at once both risked and affirmed. Will the female void swallow him up, consume him, engulf and destroy his penis, his whole self? Will the female void pollute his virile positivity with its noxious negativity? Will the female void contaminate his tenuous maleness with the overwhelming toxicity of its femaleness? Or will he emerge from the terrifying emptiness of the female's anatomical gaping hole intact—his positivity reified because, even when inside her, he managed to maintain the polarity of male and female by maintaining the discreteness and integrity of his steel-like rod; his masculinity affirmed because he did not in fact merge with her and in so doing lose himself, he did not dissolve into her, he did not become her nor did he become like her, he was not subsumed by her.

This dangerous journey into the female void must be undertaken again and again, compulsively, because masculinity is nothing in and of itself; in and of itself it does not exist; it has reality only over and against, or in contrast to, female negativity. Masculinity can only be experienced, achieved, recognized, and embodied in opposition to femininity. When men posit sex, violence, and death as elemental erotic truths, they mean this—that sex, or fucking, is the act which enables them to experience their own reality, or identity, or masculinity most concretely; that violence, or sadism, is the means by which they actualize that reality, or identity, or masculinity; and that death, or negation, or nothingness, or contamination by the female is what they risk each time they penetrate into what they imagine to be the emptiness of the female hole.

What then is behind the claim that fucking is pleasurable

for the male? How can an act so saturated with the dread of loss of self, of loss of penis, be pleasurable? How can an act so obsessive, so anxiety-ridden, be characterized as pleasurable?

First, it is necessary to understand that this is precisely the fantasy dimension of pornography. In the rarefied environs of male pornography, male dread is excised from the act of fucking, censored, edited out. The sexual sadism of males rendered so vividly in pornography is real; women experience it daily. Male domination over and against female flesh is real; women experience it daily. The brutal uses to which female bodies are put in pornography are real; women suffer these abuses on a global scale, day after day, year after year, generation after generation. What is not real, what is fantasy, is the male claim at the heart of pornography that fucking is for them an ecstatic experience, the ultimate pleasure, an unmixed blessing, a natural and easy act in which there is no terror, no dread, no fear. Nothing in reality documents this claim. Whether we examine the slaughter of the nine million witches in Europe which was fueled by the male dread of female carnality, or examine the phenomenon of rape which exposes fucking as an act of overt hostility against the female enemy, or investigate impotence which is the involuntary inability to enter the female void, or trace the myth of the *vagina dentata* (the vagina full of teeth) which is derived from a paralyzing fear of female genitalia, or isolate menstrual taboos as an expression of male terror, we find that in real life the male is obsessed with his fear of the female, and that this fear is most vivid to him in the act of fucking.

Second, it is necessary to understand that pornography is a kind of propaganda designed to convince the male that he need not be afraid, that he is not afraid; to shore him up so that he can fuck; to convince him that fucking is an unalloyed joy; to obscure for him the reality of his own terror by providing a pornographic fantasy of pleasure which he can learn as a creed and from which he can act to dominate women as a real man must. We might say that in pornography the whips, the chains, and the other paraphernalia of brutality are security blankets which give the lie to the pornographic claim that fucking issues from manhood like light from the sun. But in life, even the systematized abuse of women and the global subjugation of women to men is not sufficient to stem the terror inherent for the male in the act of fucking.

Third, it is necessary to understand that what *is* experienced by the male as authentic pleasure is the affirmation of his own identity as a male. Each time he survives the peril of entering the female void, his masculinity is reified. He has proven both that he is not her and that he is like other hims. No pleasure on earth matches the pleasure of having proven himself *real*, positive and not negative, a man and not a woman, a bona fide member of the group which holds dominion over all other living things.

Fourth, it is necessary to understand that under the sexual system of male positivity and female negativity, there is literally nothing in the act of fucking, except accidental clitoral friction, which recognizes or actualizes the real eroticism of the female, even as it has survived under slave conditions. Within the confines of the male-positive system, this eroticism does not exist. After all, a negative is a negative is a negative. Fucking is entirely a male act designed to affirm the reality and power of the phallus, of masculinity. For women, the pleasure in being fucked is the masochistic pleasure of experiencing self-negation. Under the male-positive system, the masochistic pleasure of self-negation is both mythicized and mystified in order to compel women to believe that we experience fulfillment in selflessness, pleasure in pain, validation in self-sacrifice, femininity in submission to masculinity. Trained from birth to conform to the requirements of this peculiar world view, punished severely when we do not learn masochistic submission well enough, entirely encapsulated inside the boundaries of the male-positive system, few women ever experience themselves as real in and of themselves. Instead, women are real to themselves to the degree that they identify with and attach themselves to the positivity of males. In being fucked, a woman attaches herself to one who is real to himself and vicariously experiences reality, such as it is, through him; in being fucked, a woman experiences the masochistic pleasure of her own negation which is perversely articulated as the fulfillment of her femininity.

Now, I want to make a crucial distinction—the distinction between truth and reality. For humans, reality is *social*; reality is whatever people at a given time believe it to be. In saying this, I do not mean to suggest that reality is either whimsical or accidental. In my view, reality is always a function of politics in general and sexual politics in particular—that is, it serves the powerful by fortifying and justifying their right to domination over the powerless. Reality is whatever premises social and cultural institutions are built on. Reality is also the rape, the whip, the fuck, the hysterectomy, the clitoridectomy, the mastectomy, the bound foot, the high-heel shoe, the corset, the make-up, the veil, the assault and battery, the degradation and mutilation in their concrete manifestations. Reality is enforced by those whom it serves so that it appears to be self-evident. Reality is self-perpetuating, in that the cultural and social institutions built on its premises also embody and enforce those premises. Literature, religion, psychology, education, medicine, the science of biology as currently understood, the social sciences, the nuclear family, the nation-state, police, armies, and civil law—all embody the given reality and enforce it on us. The given reality is, of course, that there are two sexes, male and female; that these two sexes are opposite from each other, polar; that the male is inherently positive and the female inherently negative; and that the positive and negative poles of human existence unite naturally into a harmonious whole.

Truth, on the other hand, is not nearly so accessible as reality. In my view, truth is absolute in that it does exist and it can be found. Radium, for instance, always existed; it was always true that radium existed; but radium did not figure in the human notion of reality until Marie and Pierre Curie isolated it. When they did, the human notion of reality had to change in fundamental ways to accommodate the truth of radium. Similarly, the earth was always a sphere; this was always true; but until Columbus sailed west to find the East, it was not real. We might say that truth does exist, and that it is the human project to find it so that reality can be based on it.

I have made this distinction between truth and reality in order to enable me to say something very simple: *that while the system of gender polarity is real, it is not true*. It is not true that there are two sexes which are discrete and opposite, which are polar, which unite naturally and self-evidently into a harmonious whole. It is not true that the male embodies both positive and neutral human qualities and potentialities in contrast to the female who is female, according to Aristotle and all of male culture, "by virtue of a certain *lack* of qualities." And once we do not accept the notion that men are positive and women are negative, we are essentially rejecting the notion that there are men and women at all. In other words, the system based on this polar model of existence is absolutely real; but the model itself is not true. We are living imprisoned inside a pernicious delusion, a delusion on which all reality as we know it is predicated.

In my view, those of us who are women inside this system of reality will never be free until the delusion of sexual polarity is destroyed and until the system of reality based on it is eradicated entirely from human society and from human memory. This is the notion of cultural transformation at the heart of feminism. This is the revolutionary possibility inherent in the feminist struggle.

As I see it, our revolutionary task is to destroy phallic identity in men and masochistic nonidentity in women—that is, to destroy the polar realities of men and women as we now know them so that this division of human flesh into two camps—one an armed camp and the other a concentration camp—is no longer possible. Phallic identity is real and it must be destroyed. Female masochism is real and it must be destroyed. The cultural institutions which embody and enforce those interlocked aberrations—for instance, law, art, religion, nation-states, the family, tribe, or commune based on father-right—these institutions are real and they must be destroyed. If they are not, we will be consigned as women to perpetual inferiority and subjugation.

I believe that freedom for women must begin in the repudiation of our own masochism. I believe that we must destroy in ourselves the drive to masochism at its sexual roots. I believe that we must establish our own authenticity, individually and among ourselves—to experience it, to create from it, and also to deprive men of occasions for reifying the lie of manhood over and against us. I believe that ridding ourselves of our own deeply entrenched masochism, which takes so many tortured forms, is the first priority; it is the first deadly blow that we can strike against systematized male dominance. In effect, when we succeed in excising masochism from our own personalities and constitutions, we will be cutting the male life line to power over and against us, to male worth in contradistinction to female degradation, to male identity posited on brutally enforced female negativity—we will be cutting the male life line to manhood itself. Only when manhood is dead—and it will perish when ravaged femininity no longer sustains it—only then will we know what it is to be free.

Notes

1. Feminism, Art, and My Mother Sylvia

1. Joseph Chaikin, *The Presence of the Actor* (New York: Atheneum, 1972), p. 126.
2. Theodore Roethke, "The Poetry of Louise Bogan," *On the Poet and His Craft: Selected Prose of Theodore Roethke*, ed. Ralph J. Mills (Seattle: University of Washington Press, 1965), pp. 133–134.

2. Renouncing Sexual "Equality"

1. Kate Millett, *Sexual Politics* (Garden City, N.Y.: Doubleday & Company, Inc., 1970).
2. Mary Jane Moffat and Charlotte Painter, eds., *Revelations: Diaries of Women* (New York: Random House, 1974), pp. 143–144.

3. Remembering the Witches

1. Heinrich Kramer and James Sprenger, *Malleus Maleficarum*, trans. M. Summers (New York: Dover Publications, Inc., 1971), p. 44.
2. *Ibid.*, p. 43.
3. *Ibid.*, p. 47.

4. *Ibid.*
5. *Ibid.*, p. 121.

4. The Rape Atrocity and the Boy Next Door

1. Sigmund Freud, "Femininity," *Women and Analysis*, ed. Jean Strouse (New York: Grossman Publishers, 1974), p. 90.
2. *The Jerusalem Bible* (Garden City, N.Y.: Doubleday & Company, Inc., 1966), pp. 243–244.
3. *Ibid.*, p. 245.
4. Cited by Carol V. Horos, *Rape* (New Canaan, Conn.: Tobey Publishing Co., Inc., 1974), p. 3.
5. Cited by Andra Medea and Kathleen Thompson, *Against Rape* (New York: Farrar, Straus & Giroux, Inc., 1974), p. 27.
6. Horos, *op. cit.*, p. 6.
7. William Matthews, *The Ill-Framed Knight: A Skeptical Inquiry into the Identity of Sir Thomas Malory* (Berkeley: University of California Press, 1966), p. 17.
8. Medea and Thompson, *op. cit.*, p. 13.
9. "Forcible and Statutory Rape: An Exploration of the Operation and Objectives of the Consent Standard," *The Yale Law Journal*, LXII (December 1952), pp. 52–83.
10. *Ibid.*, pp. 72–73.
11. Medea and Thompson, *op. cit.*, p. 26.
12. Mary Daly, *Beyond God the Father: Toward a Philosophy of Women's Liberation* (Boston: Beacon Press, 1973), pp. 8, 9, 33, 37, 47–49, 100, 106, 167.
13. New York Radical Feminists, *Rape: The First Sourcebook for Women*, eds. Noreen Connell and Cassandra Wilson (New York: New American Library, 1974), p. 165.
14. *Ibid.*
15. Medea and Thompson, *op. cit.*, p. 16.
16. The Institute for Sex Research, *Sex Offenders* (New York: Harper & Row, 1965), p. 205.
17. Menachim Amir, *Patterns of Forcible Rape* (Chicago: University of Chicago Press, 1971), p. 314.
18. Susan Griffin, "Rape: The All-American Crime," *Ramparts*, X (September 1971), p. 27.
19. Amir, *op. cit.*, p. 52.
20. Amir, *op. cit.*, p. 57.
21. Federal Bureau of Investigation, *Uniform Crime Reports*, 1974 (Washington, D.C.: Government Printing Office, 1974), p. 22.
22. Horos, *op. cit.*, p. 24.
23. Federal Bureau of Investigation, *op. cit.*, p. 24.
24. Medea and Thompson, *op. cit.*, p. 134.
25. Amir, *op. cit.*, pp. 234–235; Medea and Thompson, *op. cit.*, p. 29.
26. Medea and Thompson, *op. cit.*, p. 135.

27. Amir, *op. cit.*, p. 142.
28. Horos, *loc. cit.*
29. Medea and Thompson, *op. cit.*, p. 12.
30. Sgt. Henry T. O'Reilly, New York City Police Department Sex Crimes Analysis Unit, quoted in Joyce Wadler, "Cop, Students Talk About Rape," *New York Post*, CLXXIV (May 10, 1975), p. 7.
31. Horos, *op. cit.*, p. 13.
32. Elizabeth Gould Davis, "Too Terrible for Male Law," *Majority Report*, IV (June 27, 1974), p. 6.
33. Amir, *op. cit.*, p. 200.
34. Medea and Thompson, *op. cit.*, pp. 34–35.
35. Robert Sam Anson, "That Championship Season," *New Times*, III (September 20, 1974), pp. 46–51.
36. *Ibid.*, p. 48.
37. Angelina Grimké, speaking before the Massachusetts State Legislature, 1838, cited in Gerda Lerner, *The Grimké Sisters from South Carolina: Pioneers for Woman's Rights and Abolition* (New York: Schocken Books, 1971), p. 8.
38. Eldridge Cleaver, *Soul on Ice* (New York: Dell Publishing Co., Inc., 1968), p. 26.
39. New York Radical Feminists, *op. cit.*, pp. 164–169.
40. George Gilder, *Sexual Suicide* (New York: Quadrangle, 1973), p. 18.
41. Ida Husted Harper, *The Life and Work of Susan B. Anthony: Including Public Addresses, Her Own Letters and Many from Her Contemporaries During Fifty Years*, 3 vols. (Indianapolis and Kansas City: The Bowen-Merrill Company, 1898), I: 366.

5. The Sexual Politics of Fear and Courage

1. Simone de Beauvoir, *The Second Sex* (New York: Bantam Books, 1970), pp. xv–xvi.
2. Sigmund Freud, "Some Psychical Consequences of the Anatomical Distinction Between the Sexes," *Women and Analysis*, ed. Jean Strouse (New York: Grossman Publishers, 1974), pp. 20–21.
3. Erik Erikson, "Womanhood and Inner Space," *Identity, Youth and Crisis* (New York: W. W. Norton, 1968), pp. 277–278.
4. Andrea Dworkin, *Woman Hating* (New York: E. P. Dutton & Co., Inc., 1974), pp. 47–49.
5. Sigmund Freud, "Femininity," *Women and Analysis*, ed. Jean Strouse (New York: Grossman Publishers, 1974), p. 91.
6. See Shulamith Firestone, *The Dialectic of Sex: The Case for Feminist Revolution* (New York: Bantam Books, 1972), pp. 41–71.
7. See Dworkin, *op. cit.*, pp. 95–116.
8. Evelyn Reed, *Woman's Evolution* (New York: Pathfinder Press, Inc., 1975), p. 48.
9. Dworkin, *op. cit.*, pp. 153–154, 174–193.

8. Our Blood: The Slavery of Women in Amerika

1. George Eliot, *Felix Holt* (Harmondsworth: Penguin Books, 1972), p. 84.
2. *The Lawes Resolutions of Women's Rights: Or, the Lawes Provision for Women* (London, 1632), cited by Julia Cherry Spruill, *Women's Life and Work in the Southern Colonies* (New York: W. W. Norton & Co., Inc., 1972), p. 340.
3. Phyllis Chesler, conversation with the author.
4. Sarah Grimké, "Education of Women," essay, Box 21, Weld MSS, cited by Gerda Lerner, *The Grimké Sisters from South Carolina: Pioneers for Woman's Rights and Abolition* (New York: Schocken Books, 1974), p. 29.
5. Sarah Grimké, diary, 1827, Weld MSS, cited by Lerner, *op. cit.*, p. 23.
6. Angelina Grimké, diary, 1829, cited by Betty L. Fladeland, "Grimké, Sarah Moore and Angelina Emily," *Notable American Women: A Biographical Dictionary*, ed. Edward T. James (Cambridge, Mass.: The Belknap Press of Harvard University Press, 1974), II: 97.
7. Lerner, *op. cit.*, pp. 123–124.
8. Angelina Grimké, "An Appeal to the Christian Women of the South," *The Oven Birds: American Women on Womanhood 1820–1920*, ed. Gail Parker (Garden City, N.Y.: Anchor Books, 1972), p. 137.
9. *Ibid.*, pp. 127–129.
10. Angelina Grimké, *Letters to Catherine Beecher*, in *The Feminist Papers: From Adams to de Beauvoir*, ed. Alice S. Rossi (New York: Bantam Books, 1974), p. 322.
11. *Ibid.*, p. 320.
12. A. E. Grimké, "An Appeal to the Women of the Nominally Free States: Issued by an Anti-Slavery Convention of American Women & Held by Adjournment from the 9th to the 12th of May, 1837," cited by Lerner, *op. cit.*, pp. 162–163.
13. From a pastoral letter, "The General Association of Massachusetts (Orthodox) to the Churches Under Their Care," 1837, *The Feminist Papers: From Adams to de Beauvoir*, ed. Alice S. Rossi (New York: Bantam Books, 1974), pp. 305–306.
14. Angelina Grimké, *Letters of Theodore Dwight Weld, Angelina Grimké Weld and Sarah Grimké*, eds. Gilbert H. Barnes and Dwight L. Dumond, 1934, cited by Fladeland, *op. cit.*, p. 98.
15. Sarah Grimké, *Letters on the Equality of the Sexes and the Condition of Women*, in *The Feminist Papers: From Adams to de Beauvoir*, ed. Alice S. Rossi (New York: Bantam Books, 1974), p. 307.
16. Frederick Douglass, editorial from *The North Star*, in *Feminism: The Essential Historical Writings*, ed. Miriam Schneir (New York: Vintage Books, 1972), pp. 84–85.
17. Elizabeth Cady Stanton, *Eighty Years and More: Reminiscences 1815–1897* (New York: Schocken Books, 1973), pp. 240–241.

18. *Ibid.*, p. 255.

19. Sojourner Truth, "Keeping the Thing Going While Things Are Stirring," speech, 1867, *Feminism: The Essential Historical Writings*, ed. Miriam Schneir (New York: Vintage Books, 1972), p. 129.

BIBLIOGRAPHY

Bloomer, D. C. *Life and Writings of Amelia Bloomer*. New York: Schocken Books, 1975.

Brown, Connie, and Seitz, Jane. "'You've Come A Long Way, Baby': Historical Perspectives," *Sisterhood Is Powerful*. Edited by Robin Morgan. New York: Vintage Books, 1970. Pp. 3–28.

Bradford, Sarah. *Harriet Tubman: The Moses of Her People*. Secaucus, N.J.: The Citadel Press, 1974.

Conrad, Earl. *Harriet Tubman: Negro Soldier and Abolitionist*. New York: International Publishers, 1973.

Douglass, Frederick. *Narrative of the Life of Frederick Douglass*. Edited by Benjamin Quarles. Cambridge, Mass.: The Belknap Press of Harvard University Press, 1971.

———. *Frederick Douglass: Selections from His Writings*. Edited by Philip S. Foner. New York: International Publishers, 1971.

Duniway, Abigail Scott. *Path Breaking: An Autobiographical History of the Equal Suffrage Movement in Pacific Coast States*. New York: Schocken Books, 1971.

Firestone, Shulamith. "The Women's Rights Movement in the U.S.: A New View," *Voices from Women's Liberation*. Edited by Leslie B. Tanner. New York: New American Library, 1970. Pp. 433–443.

Fladeland, Betty L. "Grimké, Sarah Moore and Angelina Emily," *Notable American Women: A Biographical Dictionary*. Edited by Edward T. James. Cambridge, Mass.: The Belknap Press of Harvard University Press, 1974. Vol. II, pp. 97–99.

Flexner, Eleanor. *Century of Struggle: The Woman's Rights Movement in the United States*. New York: Atheneum, 1973.

Fogel, Robert William, and Engerman, Stanley L. *Time on the Cross: The Economics of American Negro Slavery*. Boston: Little, Brown and Company, 1974.

Frazier, E. Franklin. *The Negro Family in the United States*. Chicago: The University of Chicago Press, 1966.

Genovese, Eugene D. *The Political Economy of Slavery: Studies in the Economy and Society of the Slave South*. New York: Vintage Books, 1967.

———. *The World the Slaveholders Made: Two Essays in Interpretation*. New York: Vintage Books, 1971.

Gilman, Charlotte Perkins. *Women and Economics*. Edited by Carl Degler. New York: Harper Torchbooks, 1966.

Hole, Judith, and Levine, Ellen. "The First Feminists," *Notes from the Third Year*. 1971. Pp. 5–10.

Katz, William Loren, ed. *Five Slave Narratives*. New York: Arno Press, 1969.

Kraditor, Aileen S., ed. *Up from the Pedestal: Selected Writings in the History of American Feminism*. Chicago: Quadrangle Books, 1968.

———. *The Ideas of the Woman Suffrage Movement 1890–1920*. Garden City, N.Y.: Anchor Books, 1971.

Lerner, Gerda, ed. *Black Women in White America: A Documentary History*. New York: Vintage Books, 1973.

———. *The Grimké Sisters from South Carolina: Pioneers for Woman's Rights and Abolition*. New York: Schocken Books, 1974.

Parker, Gail, ed. *The Oven Birds: American Women on Womanhood 1820–1920*. Garden City, N.Y.: Anchor Books, 1972.

Petry, Ann. *Harriet Tubman: Conductor on the Underground Railroad*. New York: Pocket Books, 1973.

Rossi, Alice S., ed. *The Feminist Papers: From Adams to de Beauvoir*. New York: Bantam Books, 1974.

Schneir, Miriam, ed. *Feminism: The Essential Historical Writings*. New York: Vintage Books, 1972.

Spruill, Julia Cherry. *Women's Life and Work in the Southern Colonies*. New York: W. W. Norton & Company, Inc., 1972.

Stanton, Elizabeth Cady. *Eighty Years and More: Reminiscences 1815–1897*. New York: Schocken Books, 1973.

Tanner, Leslie B., ed. *Voices from Women's Liberation*. New York: New American Library, 1970.

Wells, Ida B. *Crusade for Justice: The Autobiography of Ida B. Wells*. Edited by Alfreda M. Duster. Chicago: The University of Chicago Press, 1970.

9. The Root Cause

1. Simone de Beauvoir, *The Second Sex* (New York: Bantam Books, 1970), pp. xv–xvi.